Visions of the Night

Visions of the Night

A Study of Jewish Dream Interpretation

JOEL COVITZ

SHAMBHALA
Boston & London
1990

Shambhala Publications, Inc.
Horticultural Hall
300 Massachusetts Avenue
Boston, Massachusetts 02115

Shambhala Publications, Inc.
Random Century House
20 Vauxhall Bridge Road
London SW1V 2SA

9 8 7 6 5 4 3 2 1

First Edition

Printed in the United States of America on acid-free paper

Distributed in the United States by Random House
and in Canada by Random House of Canada Ltd.
Distributed in the United Kingdom by Random Century Group.

Library of Congress Cataloging-in-Publication Data

Covitz, Joel, 1943–
Visions of the night : a study of Jewish dream interpretation / Joel Covitz.
p. cm.
ISBN 0-87773-448-8
1. Dreams—Religious aspects—Judaism. 2. Dreams in the Bible. I. Title.
BF1078.C67 1989 89-42631
154.6′34′089924—dc20 CIP

To Rabbi Solomon Almoli

Contents

Preface

The famous Chasidic rabbi Nachman of Bratslav said that every author should weigh his book to determine if it has any connection with the "Book of Humanity"—that is, whether humanity will receive any benefit from it. I hope that this book will contribute some helpful principles and insights to the healing work of psychotherapy. The perspective on dream interpretation offered here is a combination of my experience as a Jungian analyst, my own personal dreamwork, and my background in Jewish studies. This book is not a scholarly or historical treatment of Jewish dream theory but a more personal approach that seeks to embroider ancient wisdom into a modern practice of psychotherapy. Although I do not try to prove the acceptability of these ideas from a religious point of view, I hope that readers will share my appreciation for the Jewish contribution to this field and for the notion of dream interpretation as an honorable religious profession among the Jews.

Acknowledgments

This little book has a long line of acknowledgments. They begin with my grandfather, Rabbi Abraham Klein, whom I loved like a father and who loved me as the son he never had (he had three daughters). From him I learned to search my Jewish roots for worldly wisdom. My grandmother, Kate Klein, taught me the magical potential of life and notions of things such as angelic visitations, and reincarnation, and the interactions between people and God.

I began working on this book twenty years ago when I found my first complete edition of Solomon Almoli's book, *Pitron Chalomot,* in the Staatsbibliothek in Zurich. The translation of the first section of Almoli's treatise that I made for my diploma thesis at the C. G. Jung Institute in Zurich served as a foundation for this book. With the assistance of Medora Van Denburgh, an abridged version of that translation was put into readable English without overly sacrificing the original literal sense.

I want to thank my daughter, Susan, for editing the first draft of the manuscript. My son Daniel's "You can do it" attitude made the completion of this book an imperative. David Porat, an engineer by profession but a scholar of Jewish literature at heart, assisted me in translations of mystical texts and legends. He was also greatly helpful in finding the sources of numerous quotes that were alluded to but unidentified in Almoli's text. Efrat Porat pointed out many interesting quotes on the role of materialism in Jewish life as found in biblical and talmudic sources.

Jeremiah Abrams was a constant companion, reader of various drafts, and inspirer on this project. My brother, Howard Covitz, a Freudian analyst, assisted me with the quotes from Freud. I spent many a Sunday brunch with Phillip Nyman munching over the role of Jewish history in the formation of Jewish dream theory and the role of individual consciousness in Jewish life. Risa Neiman helped me to find the right English word in many passages.

I gratefully acknowledge Samuel Bercholz, the publisher of Shambhala Publications. Sam first approached me with the idea of writing a book on the male midlife crisis but then allowed me to fullfill my own midlife fantasy of bringing Almoli's sixteenth-century dream theory to the attention of a modern readership.

Kendra Crossen, an editor at Shambhala, worked with me throughout the formation of this book. She was never simply a slashdash editor but from the outset literally fashioned this book with her keen insight, feminine awareness, and mystical knowledge of Judaism.

This book could not have been written without the insights I have gathered in working with my patients, whom I gratefully acknowledge and to whom I express my appreciation for sharing their life experiences with me and allowing me to use some of them in this book. In order to protect the anonymity of these patients, I have changed many biographical details. I have not presented any lengthy cases, as I believe that every dream and dreamer is individually unique, which makes the practice of dream intepretation an art.

Finally, I want to thank my wife, Deborah, for her patience and encouragement during this labor of love for the last twenty years, so that I was able to fulfill a dream and a promise to myself to see the magical, mystical texts of the Jews find a meaningful place in the theory and practice of dream interpretation today.

There is no dream without its interpretation.

—*Midrash*

Visions of the Night

1. Dreams in the Jewish Tradition

When I first became interested in the field of dream interpretation, I was a chaplain in the United States Army, counseling soldiers and their families in Würzburg, West Germany. During my years at the various seminaries I attended, I had grown dissatisfied with the Orthodox Jewish world and disenchanted with organized religion. I had decided to become a chaplain because I thought it would give me a chance to combine my religious background with my interest in psychology. One of the things that had disappointed me most about the Orthodox Jewish leadership was the lack of psychological understanding I had observed on the part of the seminary teachers and their intolerance of individuality and nonconformity among the students. Gradually I was moving away from traditional religious practice and toward a career as a full-time psychotherapist. Fortunately, the psychiatrist at the post was a talented Jungian-oriented therapist who utilized several interesting techniques, including dreamwork and hypnosis, and under his supervision I began to work creatively with a variety of emotional problems. Eventually I was able to make weekly pilgrimages to the C. G. Jung Institute in Zurich, in order undergo a personal Jungian analysis and study Jungian psychology while I completed my period of obligation to the army.

From the very onset of my interest in dream interpretation, I felt a need to search my own heritage for whatever wisdom it might hold in that field. I never assumed that the material I would find in Jewish literature would play a back seat to the modern dream theories developed by Freud and Jung. On the contrary, I fully expected to discover, in the words of King Solomon, that there is nothing new under the sun. And in fact I did become convinced that the ancient wisdom concerning the use of dreams to guide human life can enhance our contemporary understanding of dream interpretation in the context of psychotherapy. In particular, my study of the work of a medieval dream theorist, Solomon Almoli, revealed some startlingly modern psychological insights into the nature and purpose of dreaming, as we shall see later in this book.

My initial search uncovered scattered references to dreams in the Talmud, the Midrash, the Zohar and other kabbalistic texts, various Jewish legends, and Jewish dream books, as well as the more familiar passages in the Bible. What immediately became evident was a monumental Jewish ambivalence on the subject. On the one hand, dreams are divine communications, omens, sources of guidance, and even, in the words of the Talmud, "one-sixtieth part prophecy." On the other hand, there are false and wicked dreams, and suspicion is cast on the self-styled prophet and "dreamer of dreams"; or else dreams are simply dismissed as meaningless and of no consequence. The resistance to dream material in Judaism—I would even go so far as to call it a phobic reaction—is significant because to a great extent it persists even to this day and explains why religious leaders have never universally accepted the dream as a source of insight and knowledge. For this reason it cannot be claimed that there is an established Jewish theory of dream interpretation, although obviously I believe that one can be formulated or I would not have written this book. However, before going on to examine the positive side of Jewish thought on dreams, let's look for a moment at the basis for this phobia.

The Bible issues a strong warning against dreams in the following passage.

> If there appears among you a prophet or a dream diviner and he gives you a sign or a portent, saying "Let us follow and worship another god"—whom you have not experienced—even if the sign or portent comes true, do not heed the words of the prophet or that dream diviner. For the Lord your God is testing you to see whether you really love the Lord your God with all

> your heart and soul. Follow none but the Lord your God, and revere none but Him; observe His commandments alone, and heed only His orders; worship none but Him, and hold fast to Him. As for that prophet or dream diviner, he shall be put to death; for he urged disloyalty to the Lord your God—who freed you from the land of Egypt and who redeemed you from the house of bondage—to make you stray from the path that the Lord your God commanded you to follow. Thus you will sweep out evil from your midst. (Deut. 13: 12–16)

The fear expressed in this passage stems from a realistic appraisal of dream material, which tends to creatively reinterpret whatever it focuses upon—including ritual, law, and other aspects of religious life. During the years when I was conducting religious services as a chaplain, I had many dreams that suggested varying the conventional form of worship. In one dream, for example, the Shema—an important prayer expressing the Jews' belief in the unity of God (beginning with the words "Hear O Israel, the Lord our God, the Lord is One")—was uttered like a mantra, emphasizing the various components of this complex prayer statement. After having this dream, I introduced some elements of experimentation into the prayers I was leading. To do so was not, however, compatible with the religious orthodoxy of my training. From the traditional point of view, the idea of allowing insights from the dream of an ordinary individual to alter the divine rules and regulations or the collective decisions of the rabbinical sages is very dangerous. There *are* legitimate ways to creatively interpret religious ideas in Judaism, but the dream inspirations of ordinary people are not among them.

This resistance can be detected in some form today even among nonreligious Jews who are largely assimilated into American culture. For instance, we don't find it particularly surprising if a fundamentalist Christian minister announces on television that God told him to run for president, whereas to Jewish Americans it would be preposterous for a religious Jew to make such a claim. Tradition has it that the age of prophecy is over and that God no longer speaks intimately to human beings as He once did to the patriarchs and prophets of biblical times. According to the Talmud, since the destruction of the Holy Temple in the year 70 C.E., prophecy has been given to fools and children. Therefore, if the only dreams that are significant are the prophetic dreams, then dreams in our unprophetic world must be insignificant.

This, I believe, is why a coherent theory of dream interpretation was never able to gain credence among the Jews, although the potential framework for such a theory is clearly present in the vast treasury of Jewish literature. And so, despite a great deal of interest in dreams, a strong folk belief in the power of dreams, and the existence of professional dream interpreters among the Jews at one time (the Talmud records the presence of twenty-four such practitioners in Jerusalem), it was impossible for a legitimate field of dream interpretation to develop. The result is that today dreams have no religious significance at all in mainstream Judaism.

There is one great scholar who set forth a dream theory based on Jewish philosophy and values, and that was Solomon Almoli, a Spanish rabbi and physician who lived in Constantinople in the sixteenth century. For Almoli, God had never abandoned His revelatory relationship with humanity, and he firmly believed that dreams contained the voice of divine guidance, helping ordinary men and women to navigate their personal lives in accordance with the destiny appointed for them by God. In affirming the existence of this "inner guidance system" as a universal gift bestowed upon all of humanity, Almoli elevated the dream to a sacred position, and the dream interpreter to the status of a sacred technician—a notion for which there was no precedent at the time. In his book *Pitron Chalomot* ("The Interpretation of Dreams"), he makes brilliant use of a wide variety of Jewish sources to justify his convictions and insights, for one of his primary goals was to restore the dream to its rightful place in Jewish life.

When I first studied *Pitron Chalomot* and set out to write a psychological commentary on it as part of my diploma thesis for the C. G. Jung Institute, I was faced with the realization that

Almoli's book is already a psychological document that can stand on its own, even in the twentieth century. For this reason, in the next chapter I present an abridgment of my translation of the text so as to let Almoli speak for himself. In the chapters following, I will return to some of the themes of his book, amplifying the material with my own observations and insights drawn from my practice of Jungian analysis.

At the beginning of this chapter I suggested that a study of Jewish dream interpretation would show that there is nothing new under the sun. Oddly enough, Almoli himself seemed to think he was starting from scratch, since he declares in a foreword to his book that what he is writing is "new of new, in that its realm has been renewed." Interestingly, Freud also expressed this notion, stating that "no foundation has been laid of secure findings on which a later investigator might build; but each new writer examines the same problems afresh and begins again, as it were from the beginning."[1] The possibility for creative reinterpretation of old material for use in new circumstances is the cornerstone of Jewish scholarship and is what gives the sacred literature of a people continued relevance through changing times; for a scripture that is treated as having some original static meaning will not be blessed with longevity. Almoli's work has the potential of enlivening not only the ancient tradition from which it springs but also the psychological tradition that influences our thinking on dreams today. I hope that my observations in turn will contribute to a creative renewal of these realms.

2. A Jewish Theory of Dream Interpretation

Solomon Almoli has the distinction of having been cited by Freud in a footnote in his book *The Interpretation of Dreams*—interestingly, the same title as Almoli's own book. Freud notes, "Dream interpretation among the Jews has been discussed by Almoli (1848)." Apparently Freud was only aware of a nineteenth-century edition of Almoli's book and didn't realize that its author wrote in the sixteenth century.

Few details of Almoli's life have been recorded. According to the *Encyclopedia Judaica*, he was born in Spain sometime before 1485 and probably left when all the Jews were expelled in 1492. He spent his early years in Salonika, Greece. Before 1515 he settled in Constantinople, where he passed the remainder of his life, dying sometime after 1542. In Constantinople he served as a Jewish judge (*dayyan*) and rabbi. He apparently earned his livelihood by the practice of medicine and served as physician to the sultan.

In addition to medicine and law, Almoli was interested in philosophy in general and kabbalistic mysticism in particular. He was also the author of a study of Hebrew grammar. His wide-ranging interests make him something of a Renaissance man, an ideal person to combine the fields of religion, healing, and dream interpretation. Not much is known of his personal life except that he claimed to have been an orphan and was beset by financial difficulties and frustrated dreams of gaining recognition for his work.

Apart from his dream book, Almoli's publications were merely introductions to larger works that he was planning to write but never finished. One of the projects dearest to his heart was a general encyclopedia, a formidable undertaking but one that he hoped could be taken up by others if he should fail to complete it. Unfortunately, the Jewish scholars of Constantinople responded negatively to the idea. He did, however, publish a small pamphlet as a prospectus for the encyclopedia.

Almoli's fantasy of writing an encyclopedia is revealing about his view of the meaning of life—what we might call, in Jungian terms, his myth of individuation. He states that he wanted to write an encyclopedia because he believed that every person has approximately one great thing to say to the world in his lifetime, while the remainder of his ideas are merely echoes of other people's thoughts. Almoli wanted to gather together all the "new" ideas contained in important books, eliminating the repetitious material. In this way his encyclopedia would free people from having to spend a lifetime poring through thousands of complete volumes in their attempt to cull the one new idea contained in each one. Like the great Jewish philosopher Maimonides before him, he wanted to collate all of Jewish knowledge so as to simplify the laborious task of studying the wisdom of former generations. Almoli envisioned his encyclopedia as being the only book a Jew would have to read (apart from the Bible); individuals would thus have time to search for their own line to add to the history of ideas for the good of humanity.

It is important to realize that this fantasy would be considered to border on heresy by the typical medieval Jewish scholar. The radical implications of Almoli's idea is that the study of Torah and Talmud is not every man's life task, as it is in the traditional Jewish view, but that each person has his or her own unique quest for individual development. This is a distinctly modern idea, which no doubt explains why Almoli's effort to write such an encyclopedia was never supported by his peers.

This is not to say, however, that Almoli was unsuccessful in his work. He was about thirty years old when his dream book was first printed in Salonika in 1515, under the title *Mefasher Chelmin* ("Dream Mediator"), and it was republished under the title *Pitron Chalomot* ("The Interpretation of Dreams") in Constantinople in 1518 and 1551, in Cracow in 1576, and many times afterward, up to the twentieth century. The last complete edition of the book appeared at the end of the nineteenth century. A Yiddish version was issued as recently as 1902 in Brooklyn, New York.

The long publishing history of Almoli's book is impressive evidence of its popularity. The book "clicked." This was not a dark, esoteric volume of visions of the soul, but was designed as a people's book. In all probability it was not the sort of book to appeal to the scholarly caste of Jews, who no doubt never accepted it wholeheartedly. A sign of its being a book for the people is that its dream-dictionary section was translated into Yiddish, the mother tongue of eastern European Jewry. This indicates that it was seen as a woman's book, since traditionally Jewish women in Europe did not study Hebrew but could read Yiddish. I sometimes muse to myself that Almoli's book must have been waiting for the women's movement to come along before it could gain any attention in English translation. Today our culture is witnessing a reawakening of appreciation for the feminine principle, which allows for the possibility of God's maintaining a living relationship to individuals through dreams, intuitions, and visions.

Pitron Chalomot consists of three sections. The first part sets forth Almoli's dream theory and principles of interpretation with the philosophical and textual sources to support them. It is this section of the book that I present in English translation, in abridged form, in this chapter. The second part of Almoli's book is a "dictionary" offering interpretations of specific dream symbols; I will discuss some of its features in chapter 3. The final section of Almoli's book discusses the religious laws pertaining to dreams, generally with the intention of "breaking the spell" of bad dreams by means of religious ritual.

About the Translation

The first part of *Pitron Chalomot* in the original Hebrew text is at times heavy, polemical, repetitive, and even boring—an indication of the laborious task of a medieval Jewish philosopher who had to work within a tradition. Much of the material could be described as an obsessional search through the Jewish literature for passages that would justify Almoli's personal vision of dream interpretation. In abridging the text, I have sought to spare the reader the obsessiveness while preserving the most important and interesting insights. The text is translated freely with the aim of making it "friendly" to the modern reader. The spirit, however, is Almoli's, and I have not altered his ideas nor added anything substantive to them.

In the sixteenth century, Hebrew books were written without any punctuation, footnotes, or citations. Almoli assumed that his readers would be familiar with the sources he was quoting, which included not only the Bible but also the Talmud, Midrash, Zohar, and works of medieval Jewish philosophers. For the benefit of the modern reader, I have looked up as many sources as I could and added the citations in parentheses to the text.

THE INTERPRETATION OF DREAMS

Introduction

Man, yearning ever toward an understanding of the essence of all things, desires to know, whether for good or for ill, that which has been preordained for this world. But by virtue of his humanity, man is incapable of attaining such understanding on his own. Therefore, the Providence of the Lord comes to his aid, as divine inspiration, taking the form of either prophecy or dream. In truth, nothing comes about in this world that was not first announced from on high, as we find in the Zohar:

> Nothing takes place in the world but what has previously been made known, either by means of a dream, or by means of a proclamation, for it has been affirmed that before any event comes to pass in the world, it is first announced in heaven, whence it is proclaimed to the world. Thus Scripture states, "For the Lord God will do nothing but he reveals His counsel unto His servants the prophets" (Amos 3:7). This refers to the time when there were yet prophets in the world; when the prophets were no more, they were succeeded by the sages. And, in our time, when the sages too are no longer among us, that which is still to come is revealed in dreams, or, if not in dreams, through the medium of the birds of the heavens. And so we have laid down. (Gen., *Vayeshev* 183b)

Since the time of our exile from our homeland Israel, prophecy came to an end, and the Urim and Tumim [oracle] was hidden from us. Yet, even so, we have retained our ability to be inspired by dreams, which tell us of all that will come to pass. This idea is to be found in the Talmud:

> Rabbah said, "Although the Holy One, blessed be He, said, 'And I will surely hide My face in that day' (Deut. 31:18), He also said, 'I do speak with him in a dream' (Num. 12:6)." (*Chagigah* 5b)

But despite the blessing of hearing the voice of God in our dreams, we still are unsatisfied. For the content of our dreams overwhelms us, so that we fail to comprehend what we hear. The causes of this condition are various. To begin with, we are not versed in the fundamentals of inquiry. It can also be hard to understand the numerous symbolic representations inhabiting our dreams, in forms bizarre and unique, as when an image appears to be analogous to many different things at the same time. It is equally difficult to discover and to differentiate from among their fellows strong men with the intuitive power and other attributes necessary to the practice of dream interpretation. There is in addition the problem of useless material that we find interwoven in the dream. Moreover, since the subject matter of dreams is virtually infinite, a scholarly treatise can discuss the topic in only a general, if not a superficial, manner. The minutest details are forever obscured from the eyes of the interpreter. The only means of comprehension is through intuition and speculation, and even this method is fraught with error. Avuchemed demonstrated this notion when he wrote that the interpretation of dreams is possible only by means of intuition and that mistakes are common.

And behold, in spite of the endless bounty of heaven, which would make everything known to us without hindrance, we are blind to this inspiration because of our neglect of study and our failure to understand. Elihu took note of this failure, saying [in response to Job],

> Why do you contend against Him, saying, "He will answer none of my words"? For God speaks in one way, and in two, though man does not perceive it. In a dream, in a vision of the night, when deep sleep falls upon men, while they slumber on their beds; then He opens the ears of men, and through their chastisements He seals their decree, that men

may put away their purpose, and that He may hide pride from man. (Job 33:13–17)

These words signify that from the standpoint of the Holy One, blessed be He, He has already whispered into our ears as we lay dreaming, but from our point of view the manner of His revelation is closed and sealed, and we do not understand it.

Thus it was that in earlier times there were persons deeply learned in the wisdom of dreams, who were sought out by those who dreamed, so that the true messages of their dreams might be made known to them, and that in this way the divine communication would not be wasted.

It is not given to all to have the power to penetrate into the hidden words of dreams. There might be but one in a city or two in a family.[1] This was the case with Joseph, Daniel, Rabbi Ishmael, Bar Hedya, and the twenty-four dream interpreters of Jerusalem, as mentioned in the Talmud. Jerusalem was a place of divine inspiration; when the Shekhinah [Divine Presence] of God and the Ark of the Covenant yet resided in the city, there were to be found within its gates a great number of highly reputed dream interpreters. Into each generation were born wise men who excelled in this special knowledge and who comprehended the subject matter of dreams, so that those who consulted these interpreters learned from their dreams and therefore dreamed to meaningful ends.

This may have been the intention of Joseph when he said, "Do not interpretations belong to God [Elohim]?" (Gen. 40:8). *Elohim*, in this context, does not refer to God but is employed in the sense of a person of wisdom and higher understanding, as in the verse "And the Lord said unto Moses: 'See, I have set you in God's stead [as Elohim] to Pharaoh' " (Exod. 7:1). We might well say that without wisdom there can be no interpretation.

The subtlety of this wisdom and the difficulty of acquiring it have discouraged people from taking up this profession, so that

[1] The expression "one in a city or two in a family" is paradoxical, as one would expect the opposite to be true. This seems to have been a pet expression of Almoli's.

in the state of sin in which we find ourselves today, God's precious words remain as uninterpreted visions.

One wonders why learned men of the past wrote on every imaginable topic, yet not one composed a book on dream interpretation. And when we do find the matter spoken of, it is in a deprecating manner. Behold, we learn from the Talmud that Bar Hedya possessed a special book dealing with the interpretation of dreams: "He let fall a book. Rabbah found it, and saw written in it: 'All dreams follow the mouth' " (*Berakhot* 56a). What is even harder for me to comprehend is that the whole world seems to dismiss dreams as being useless things and to speak of them as having no consequence, as if they were not real; they see dreams as mere metaphors.

Therefore, observing all this, I, Solomon Almoli, the most insignificant of my generation, became imbued with zeal for God, the God of the prophets and of His people Israel, in order that His communications to us should not be lost. I took it upon myself to seek out every word written upon this subject and then to transcribe these sayings, together with my own meager contributions, into a single small text that will bloom like a rose. Ultimately it will find itself in the hands of the whole people because "it is time to be gracious unto her" (Ps. 102:14). I have titled this book "Dream Mediator" [later changed to "The Interpretation of Dreams"], for I will set forth universally valid principles whereby all people will be able to interpret their dreams and understand their significance.

The First Gate

The aim of the first gate is to clearly define the various types of dreams and to differentiate among them. The definition of the dream according to the philosopher[2] is the seeing of resemblances during sleep, which includes three levels of dreams, each being higher than the next.

[2] Maimonides, or Moses ben Maimon (1135–1204), the great philosopher of Judaism and codifier of biblical and talmudic laws.

The first level, the highest of all, is that of the prophetic dream, such as the dream of Jacob, Daniel, and Solomon. Their dreams were, without question, prophetic dreams and as such surpass ordinary dreams, which are only one-sixtieth part prophetic (see Talmud, *Berakoth* 57b).

The second level—that of ordinary dreams, like the dreams of Joseph, Pharaoh, and Pharaoh's servants, as well as the dreams of Avimelech (Gen. 20) and Laban the Aramite (Gen. 31)—is not prophetic.

The third level is that of the dreams of sorcerers and false prophets, such as those whom the Torah describes as "a dreamer of dreams" (Deut. 13:2) or, as Jeremiah says, "I have heard what the false prophets prophesy in My name, falsely saying, 'I have dreamed, I have dreamed,' who try to cause My people to forget My name by their dreams which they tell one another" (Jer. 23:25, 27). This type of dream is represented by Shemaiah ha-Nechalmi [the Nechelamite], who, I believe, was called ha-Nechalmi because the name implies that his dreams were self-induced (see Jer. 29:31–32). All of these dreams deserve only to be denounced, for their subject proves that they are neither prophetic nor ordinary, and that they are in fact magical.

And so I have laid forth the three levels of dreams. It may well be that it was to these three levels that Elihu was alluding when he stated: "For God speaks in one way, and in two." Of ordinary dreams Elihu says, "When deep sleep falls upon men." This refers to the well-known fact that ordinary dreams do not come until one is sleeping deeply. But of the third type he says, "in slumberings upon the bed," for these—may God save us from them—are the dreams of sorcerers. They come to the dreamer as a result of his own volition, to those who prepare themselves before sleeping; it could be said that such dreams are produced by the powers of the dreamer's conjuration.

Prophetic dreams can come only to those who are wise, righteous, powerful, and distinguished. Thus it seems from the intention of Scripture that in the Diaspora the Holy One, blessed be He, removed His Presence from the Israelites, His Presence which is an essential element of prophecy, without which there can be no prophecy. But dreams of the sort in which God is not present, those which come from the Master of Dreams,[3] were not withdrawn from the Jews in the Diaspora. This is the significance of the words "I do speak with him in a dream" (Num. 12:6).

There is a discourse in a book by Hasdai Crescas[4] in which he describes the difference between the ordinary dream and the prophetic dream as the strength or weakness of the power of its images. That is, in the dreams of the prophets the images possess the force of waking reality; therefore the prophet would remember what he had dreamed and could never forget it. This is not the case with an ordinary dream, whose images are weak, so that oftentimes one forgets all that he has dreamed.

By the same token, we read in the Zohar:

> Rabbi Jose, commencing the discourse, said, "For a dream comes through the multitude of business; and a fool's voice through a multitude of words" (Eccles. 5:2). As we have previously explained, dreams have various sources and may be understood at many different levels. There are dreams that are completely true, while some combine both truth and falsehood. But to those who were truly righteous, dream contents were never false but true in their entirety. Behold that which is written by Daniel: "There was the secret revealed unto Daniel in a vision of the night" (Dan. 7:1). If there were false words, why was this even entered in the Scripture? We must thereby conclude that for those who are truly righteous, when their souls ascend, only holy things adhere to them. The are informed only of matters of truth, matters that will be fulfilled that never lie! (Zohar, *Eccles.*)

This is a clear exposition of the truth that all superior dreams—those at the higher level of prophetic dreams—contain no useless material whatsoever, as is not the case with other types of dreams.

[3] The angel appointed to oversee all dreams. See chapter 3 for a discussion of Gabriel as the Master of Dreams.

[4] A Spanish Kabbalist and philosopher (died 1412).

This is true even of quite obscure dreams, as evidenced by these words from the Midrash:

> Rabbi Abbahu said, "Dreams have no influence at all. But a certain man went to Rabbi Jose ben Chalafta and said to him, "I was told in a dream, 'Go and bring the fruits of your father's labors from Cappadocia.' " "Did your father ever visit Cappadocia?" the rabbi inquired. On hearing a negative response, he said to the man, "Go and count twenty boards in the flooring of your house, and you will find what you have been ordered to seek." "But there are not twenty boards there," was the dreamer's reply. "If that is the case," said the rabbi, "count from the beginning to the end and back again, and you will find it." The dreamer went and did as he had been told, and he found his inheritance. And how did the Rabbi Jose ben Chalafta deduce this? From the word Cappadocia![5] From this dream Rabbi ben Halafta derived the rule of Bar Kapparah that "there is no dream without its interpretation." (*Gen. Rabbah, Vayetze* 68:12)

It seems that Rabbi Abbahu had thought that dreams are valueless nonsense and that this legend is presented in contradiction to this point of view. Thus the Midrash concludes with the notion of Bar Kapparah that "there is no dream without its interpretation."

In truth, however, the falsity of dreams achieved by sorcery is seen in the scriptural commentary on such dreams:

> Behold, I am against them that prophesy lying dreams (Jer. 23:32). Let not your prophets that are in the midst of you, and your diviners, beguile you, neither hearken you to your dreams which you cause to be dreamed. For they prophesy falsely unto you in My name; I have not sent them, says the Lord. (Jer. 29:8–9)

It is also stated, in reference to Shemaiah ha-Nechalmi, that he "has caused you to trust in a lie" (Jer. 29:31). Our rabbis of blessed memory have also told us that the verse "The diviners have seen a lie, and the dreams speak falsely" (Zech. 10:2) alludes

[5] In Greek, *kappa* is "twenty" and *dokia* is "boards."

to the type of dream that comes from a demon, that has its origin in sorcery.

A further distinction among dream types is that the ordinary dream does not begin in the will of the dreamer, for true dreams are the result not of one's choice but of the will of God. But the dreams of sorcerers are derived from their own choice and will. Aroused by the sorcerer's incantations, the evil spirit comes to him in a dream in an imaginary way, answering the dreamer's specific request; as Jeremiah the prophet stated, "Neither hearken you to your dreams which you cause to be dreamed." The implication is that such a person has caused himself to dream and that the contents of his dream are self-determined.

One may also distinguish among types of dreams insofar as ordinary dreams always contain some degree of truth, which is not the case with the dreams of sorcerers, whose contents are virtually all false. We must realize that "there can be no dream without some useless material" (Talmud, *Berakhot* 55a). We may understand from this that in this imperfect world, our dreams are not necessarily consistent in respect to meaningful content but invariably contain some worthless matter. But you will never come across a dream that is totally without value. If the commonly held idea subscribed to by Rabbi Moses ha-Kohen were true—namely, that the vast majority of dreams are illusory and nonsensical—then this would be the notion that we would find in the Talmud, not the concept of dreams containing merely some useless material. So we can rest assured that the reverse is also true; just as there is no dream without some useless material, so there is no dream without some useful material. If we think a dream has no significance, we may be sure that we have failed to understand the dream.

It is impossible for an ordinary dream to come from a demon, for such a dream is within the realm of prophecy, being one-sixtieth prophetic. It is thus certain that evil spirits have no place there at all, despite the fact that the ordinary dream is at a lower level than that of the prophetic dream. Therefore, we cannot but conclude that only sorcerers' dreams have a demonic source.

Now I will list some of the ways in which the impure dream may be distinguished from the pure. As I have shown, there are only two genuine forms of dreams: the prophetic and the ordinary. It may well be that it was only these two types of dreams to which Elihu referred when he said, "For God speaks in one way, and in two, though man does not perceive it." Elihu goes on to speak of "a vision of the night," or the prophetic dream, and then of the hour "when deep sleep falls upon men," the condition from which ordinary dreams arise. He ends by explaining that the purpose of the ordinary dream is "that men put away their purpose, and that He may hide pride from man." This is what I will expound upon, God willing, in the first chapter of the Fourth Gate. Of the third sort of dream, that arrived at through sorcery, Elihu does not speak, as this is not true communication.

In conclusion, one should ascribe value only to the two true forms of dream communication. It is upon these two that the words of my book will dwell. However, since the area of the prophetic dream is more profound than that of the ordinary dream, and since to speak of this requires an investigation of the phenomenon of prophecy, which no longer exists in this world, I will speak primarily of the ordinary dream, and only incidentally of the prophetic dream.

The Second Gate

The second gate will deal with the question of whether or not it is appropriate to rely upon ordinary dreams.

The First Chapter

The first chapter shows that there are no contradictory views concerning this matter.

Scripture's statements regarding the subject of dreaming are not always consistent. On the one hand, we find the Lord saying, "I do speak with him in a dream" (Num. 12:6), representative of the attitude expressed throughout the Torah that one should rely upon the truthfulness of one's dreams. The dreams of Joseph, for instance, although not prophetic, were all fulfilled; not one particle of them was lost to the ground. Even Joseph's dream about the moon (Gen. 37:9), symbolizing his [deceased] mother, Rachel, was fulfilled by his stepmother, Bilhah, who raised him as if he were her own son. Joseph's first dreams were equally significant, although their fulfillment was separate from that of the later dream. This phenomenon is found not only among the righteous (*tzaddikim*), for we see that among evil persons dreams may also speak truly of events yet to come. Pharaoh the Wicked dreamed of seven cows and seven sheaths (Gen. 41), which Joseph interpreted as referring to seven years of plenty and seven years of famine. Concerning this dream it is written, "What God is about to do He has declared unto Pharaoh" (Gen. 41:25). Truly the seven years of plenty came about in Egypt, and the seven years of famine would doubtless also have occurred, save that the great merit of Joseph diminished the decree, as our sages have laid forth in the Midrash. The dreams of Pharaoh's servants were likewise fulfilled: "And it came to pass as he [Joseph] interpreted to us" (Gen. 41:13). This was also the case with Nebuchadnezzar the Wicked, for his dreams were fulfilled as well.

Our rabbis of blessed memory have stated that "a dream is one-sixtieth part prophecy." And in the Midrash Rabbah we read that "the dream is the unripe fruit of prophecy." Furthermore, our sages were meticulous in the matter of recording dreams. For example, we find in the Talmud:

> Rabbi Chunah ben Manoach, Rabbi Samuel ben Idi, and Rabbi Chiyya of Wastanya used to attend the lectures of Rabbah. When Rabbah died, they then attended those of Rabbi Papa, and whenever he expounded to them a law with which they did not agree, they would wink at one another, which was very offensive to the older man. He subsequently found himself saying, in a dream, " 'And I cut off the three shepherds' (Zech. 11:8)."

When, on the day following, these three disciples took their leave of him, he said to them, "Go in peace."[6] (*Ta'anit* 9a–b)

The Talmud is replete with such instances. We also read that "if one has a dream that causes his soul anguish, he should go and have it turned to good" (*Berakhot* 55b).[7] It is also stated that "fasting is as efficacious for the bad dream as fire is for refuse"; upon this Rabbi Chisda commented, "And [the fast must be] on the same day [as the dream]," and Rabbi Joseph added, "Even if [the day] is the Sabbath" (*Ta'anit* 12b).[8] The Talmud is indeed rich in the exposition and interpretation of dreams. We can only ask, if dreams are insignificant, why were men of wisdom so concerned with them?

This point requires no further substantiation; reality is sufficient to reveal the truth. It is a common occurrence that one's dreams are fulfilled; we can only conclude that dreams are significant and should be attended to closely.

On the other hand, from other sources, we might derive a totally opposite point of view—that dreams are insignificant. We might consider the statements in Scripture to the effect that "the dreamers tell false dreams and give empty consolation" (Zech. 10:2) and "a dream comes through a multitude of business" (Eccl. 5:2). Even our rabbis of blessed memory have often actually stated that dreams have no significance (see Talmud, *Sanhedrin* 30a). Furthermore, we have the evidence of our own experience, which shows us numerous dreams that are never fulfilled. Even if one interprets the dream, it is still not fulfilled—not as given by the interpretation nor anything like it!

Rabbi Samuel seems to have been in doubt whether dreams are significant, leaning at times toward one opinion and at others toward the opposite:

[6] "Go in peace": the customary manner of addressing the dead, implying that the disciples were not long for this world.

[7] Maurice Simon's translation from *Berakhot* 55b: "If one has a dream which makes him sad he should go and have it interpreted in the presence of three. . . . he should have a good turn given to it in the presence of three."

[8] Normally it would be forbidden to fast on the Sabbath.

> When Samuel had a bad dream, he used to say, "Dreams speak falsely" (Zech. 10:2). But when he had a good dream, he used to say, "Do the dreams speak falsely, seeing that it is written, 'I do speak with him in a dream' (Num. 12:6)?" (Talmud, *Berakhot* 65b)

THE SECOND CHAPTER

This chapter will demonstrate that dreams are indeed genuine and in fact approach the realm of prophecy.

PART ONE

The first part will substantiate and elaborate upon this view from many angles in order to show that dream communications are divine inspirations.

The philosopher Ben Sinai writes that dreams are not caused by God, offering as proof of this assertion the fact that even creatures lacking in higher consciousness have dreams. For instance, dogs at times seem to bark in their sleep, which Aristotle interprets as a sign that they are dreaming; and it would seem unlikely that God would be present in the dreams of such creatures. However, according to our understanding of what constitutes dreaming, this is no proof whatsoever, for a dog's apparent barking while asleep is but a natural extension of its waking behavior. Similarly, we may observe that an infant may seem to be sucking in its sleep, even though its mouth is empty of the breast. And we may be sure that infants do not dream, as Ben Sinai himself admits.[9]

So it seems, in truth, that dreams share some small portion of the character of prophecy and are attributable to the influence of the Lord. That such communication is not merely coincidental is

[9] Today it is known that even fetuses exhibit REM sleep, the period of "rapid eye movement" during which dreams arise.

supported by Rabbi Levi ben Gerson's[10] statement, in his treatise *Wars of the Lord*, that what occurs as the result of chance alone occurs infrequently and is rarely found among phenomena occurring collectively.

Non-Jewish scholars contribute to the support of my view in that they report instances of waking visions that are verifiably predictive. In the terminology of such scholars the study of these events is called parapsychology. They present in their works many examples such as may be found in Greek legends. For instance, when Alexander was born, an eagle was observed perching in the courtyard of his father, King Philip. The eagle remained stationary throughout the day, crying out and spreading its wings, in the direction of the four corners of the world. This event was undoubtedly an omen of Alexander's future role as conqueror of the world. It is also said that when Plato was a mere suckling, a swarm of bees appeared one day and rested on his mouth as he lay asleep in his crib, at length ascending far aloft. This occurrence foretold Plato's great wisdom, for just as bees gather the materials, so too the wise man devotes his entire life to discovering the underlying patterns of things in order first to understand them and then to pass on to others the virtues inherent in these patterns.

It is also said that on the day that the emperor Julius Caesar died, a bird whose name was Rigatto alit in his presence and that there then appeared a host of hunters in pursuit of this bird, who slew it before Caesar's very eyes. This event was a portent of the emperor's death, for as it transpired, he was assassinated that same day by his own legions with their weapons of iron.

The irrefutable conclusion to be drawn from all these episodes is that dreams have their source in God's inspiration. Accordingly, our sages of blessed memory have said, "A dream is one-sixtieth part prophecy." Further, being that dreams are inspired by God, our sages have said, "If one goes seven days without a dream, he is called evil" (*Berakhot* 55b). The reasoning behind

[10] Levi ben Gerson (1288–1344), also known as Gersonides, was a French Jewish philosopher and physician.

this statement is that the lack of dreaming shows that one is unworthy of divine inspiration.

PART TWO

The second part will explain why dreams occur during sleep rather than when we are awake.

The fact that dreams occur during the sleeping state has already been elaborated upon by Aristotle in his *De anima*, which states that through the relaxation and inattentiveness of the physical self, one's intellectual faculties are intensified. It is well known that body and soul are opposite to one another, that what one of these chooses the other detests, each heeding its own distinct sense of direction. The body strives without ceasing to participate in the realm of material things and physical desires, while the soul turns toward the realm of the intellect. The result is that body and soul loathe each other's worlds, so that when the power of one is diminished, that of the other is strengthened. Thus we find in books on ethics that the relationship between body and soul could be compared to that of two quarrelsome women married to one man, in that when the husband is angry with one of the wives, the other wife rejoices.

I should, however, digress briefly to respond to a question put to me in contradiction to what I have stated previously. It is said that

> prophecy will not come to a person by means of either weeping or jesting but only through joy, as it is written, " 'But now bring me a minstrel.' And it came to pass, when the minstrel played, that the hand of the Lord came upon him" (2 Kings 3:15). (Talmud, *Shabbat* 30b, *Pesachim* 117a)

It is likewise related in the Talmud that the great teacher Rabbah would habitually begin his discourse with a humorous story that made his students laugh. Furthermore, in regard to Isaac's request of Esau to bring him savory food (Gen. 27:4), the biblical commentaries put forward the idea that the purpose of this savory food was to arouse Isaac to a state of joy, which in turn would inspire him to bless his son. But how can joy or pleasure be the source of prophecy? The opposite should be true, for the food should inhibit the constellation of the intellectual faculties, if we subscribe to the view that the strengthening of the body weakens the intellect.

I believe that the solution to this dilemma is that the seat of joy is not within the domain of the body but within the realm of the soul. We find that joy is attributed to the Lord, for it is stated, "Let the Lord rejoice in His works" (Ps. 104:31), and we customarily say at weddings, "Let us bless the Lord, as joy is His habitation." Therefore, when one rejoices, the power of the body is not made stronger through that joy, but, on the contrary, its strength passes into the soul and can thereby lead one into prophecy.

Jesting, on the other hand, is attributed to the realm of the body, as the body derives pleasure from such activity, which can then inhibit the intellect. Thus it is said, "Prophecy will not come to a person by means of jesting." But joy is good for a person, for we have been enjoined, "Serve the Lord with gladness" (Ps. 100:2).

The entire matter may be clarified by pointing out that although the affliction of the body enlivens the intellect, such is not the case when prophecy is involved. There the affliction of the body would in fact hinder the activation of inspiration, for prophecy comes through one's imaginative faculty, whose means of transmission is the body. Therefore it was indeed necessary for Isaac to fortify his body with the savory food in order to constellate the inspiration.

Here we find the undeniable rationale for the phenomenon of dreams occurring only during sleep and not while we are awake. As dreams are within the realm of prophecy, and as prophecy occurs only after the power of the body has been rendered void, it is only during sleep that the power of the soul speaks out with its full clarity. But if dreaming were to occur during wakefulness, prophetic inspiration could not take place unless the soul were on the verge of departing the body, as when one is at the point of death. Thus Scripture states, "neither was there breath left in me (Dan. 10:17), and "a deep sleep fell upon Abram[11] (Gen. 15:12). Inspiration could not otherwise occur, unless one's spiritual level were exalted, as in the case of Moses our Teacher, as well as that of a small number of prophets whose intellectual faculties exceeded their bodily power.

So dreams do not come during the waking state, when the body's power is overwhelmingly oppressive to the soul. Dreams come during sleep, at a time when the sensations and the body power is null: "Sleep is one-sixtieth part death" (*Berakhot* 57b). This explains the notion, found among the words of our rabbis of blessed memory, that during sleep one's soul rises into the firmament and amuses itself with the Holy One, blessed be He.

THE THIRD GATE

This gate will attempt to show how to differentiate between the true and the untrue dream.

DIFFERENTIATION BASED ON THE THOUGHTS OF THE DREAMER

It must always be borne in mind that the majority of dreams consists of representations of the dreamer's thoughts and mundane concerns. It is the responsibility of the interpreter to recognize that this type of dream is insignificant, as its source is not the Master of Dreams; it is simply the product of one's imagination. Most dreams are woven by the Spinner of Dreams from whatever the dreamer saw or thought of during the preceding day, embroidered by his imaginative powers. As we learn from

[11] Followed by a vision.

the Talmud, "If one sees a married woman in a dream, he will assuredly enter the world to come, but only if he has not thought about her during the previous day" (*Berakhot* 57a). We may infer from this passage that if the dreamer were to think about the woman during the day and consequently dream of her, the dream would be insignificant. Here is another telling instance:

> The Roman emperor said to Rabbi Joshua ben Rabbi Chananyah, "You Jews profess to be very clever, so tell me what I shall dream of tonight." The rabbi replied, "You will dream that the Persians will enslave you, despoil you, and force you to feed unclean animals while bearing a golden crook." The emperor thought of this prediction all day, and that night it all came to pass as had been foretold. Similarly, King Shapor I spoke the same words to Samuel: "You Jews profess to be very clever, so tell me what I shall dream of tonight." Samuel told the king, "You will dream that the Romans will make you a captive and put you to work grinding the pits of dates in a golden mill." After pondering on this vision all day, the king dreamed exactly what Samuel had depicted. (*Berakhot* 56a)

It would scarcely be plausible to maintain that these "predictions" were actually fulfilled at a later date. Further, if all aspects of dreams were always fulfilled, people would concentrate all day on the good things they desire, in order to dream of them during the night, so that they would eventually become reality.

In summation, we have seen the dreams that are derived from one's mundane thoughts are inconsequential. Therefore the dream interpreter must be capable of detecting in each dream any elements that do not partake of the essence of the dream, differentiating the extraneous from the essential. This, to my mind, is what is meant by Rabbi Berakhiah's statement that "while part of a dream may be fulfilled, the whole of it is never fulfilled" (Talmud, *Berakhot* 55a). This point of view is likewise implied in the scriptural passage, " 'The prophet that has a dream, let him tell a dream, and he that has My word, let him speak My word faithfully. What has the straw to do with the wheat?' says the Lord" (Jer. 23:28). The Talmud elucidates this:

> Why were the straw and the wheat spoken of in conjunction with the topic of dreams? Just as wheat cannot be without straw, so too there can be no dream without some useless material. It is written, in reference to Joseph's dream, "And, behold, the sun and the moon" (Gen. 37:9). But at that time Joseph's mother was no longer living. (*Berakhot* 55a–b)

Thus our sages implied that there are no dreams that are not interwoven with some insignificant material, as in the case of Joseph dreaming of his mother when she was already dead. In other words, his mother, symbolized by the moon, had no part in the essence of the dream. Surely he had thought and talked of her repeatedly during the prior day, filled with anxiety over her death. This tendency of dreams to contain extraneous material is, I believe, the meaning of "The dreamers tell false dreams" (Zech. 10:2), inasmuch as all dreams are mixed in with such falsities. This surely was Jeremiah's intent when he spoke of false prophets who proclaim that they transmit the words of the Lord: "Do not listen to the words of the prophets who prophesy to you with vain hopes; they speak visions of their minds, not from the mouth of the Lord" (Jer. 23:16). These false prophets relate vanities devoid of value, merely reflections of what they have thought about during the day before. This may also have been in the minds of Joseph's brothers when they told him that his dreams were insignificant (Gen. 37:10). They were implying that Joseph's dream of ruling his family resulted from his having dwelled on this subject during his waking hours. Thus the brothers said to Joseph, "Are you indeed to have dominion over us?" Onkelos translates this Aramaic text as, "You have compared yourself to a king over us," concurring with our interpretation of this passage.

We should look also to the introduction to Daniel's first dream vision, in which he "wrote the dream and told the sum of the matter" (Dan. 7:1). The meaning of this text, as explained by our teacher Sa'adiah, is that Daniel transcribed only an abbreviated form of the dream—the sum of the matter—although the dream also contained material that he did not write down. Thus we see that Daniel, who was an authentic interpreter of dreams and who knew how to separate the food from the refuse, recognized those parts of his dreams which possessed no real value and preserved only the essence of the dreams, deleting the extraneous material that derived from his thoughts during the previous day. Along the same lines, it is likely that King Solomon, in his wisdom, was alluding to this notion when he said that "a dream comes through a multitude of business" (Eccl. 5:2). Solomon was referring to the fact that dreams do not come to us in a pure state but come bearing concerns that are not essential to their interpretation.

Another example of this is to be seen in Pharaoh's dream in which he was standing on the river (Gen. 41:1); this image was not essential to the dream but referred to his thoughts during the prior day, in that he considered himself to be a god, who therefore could walk on the river. Pharaoh probably said to himself that it was his river and that he had created it, thinking of himself as a great fish in his own river. But when he related this dream to Joseph, he revised this part, saying instead that he was standing "upon the brink of the river" (Gen. 41:17), presumably being too embarrassed to reveal his megalomania to Joseph.

DIFFERENTIATION BASED ON THE LEVEL OF EXCITEMENT WITHIN A DREAM

The best means of differentiating the true from the untrue dream is by the degree of excitement experienced by the dreamer. If one dreams of powerful fantasy images that cause him to be excited or to feel anger or fear during the dream itself, this is a true dream; but if the images are insipid and arouse no strong feelings, the dream is not true. The reliability of any dream is thus in proportion to its level of excitement.

This point of view is arrived at logically, for, as was discussed in reference to prophecy, excitement occurs in a dream in order to diminish the bodily humors to the end that the intellect will be strengthened and will alone remain alert. If one becomes excited by a dream, this excitement reflects the fact that the power of the body has been lessened and the intellect is now in a better position to receive divine inspiration, as has been explained previously. When such excitement is absent, the dream will contain less that is true.

The Fourth Gate

This gate will clarify which things normally appear in dreams and which things are unusual to appear.

THE FIRST CHAPTER

This chapter will clarify whether it is possible for dreams to bode neither good nor ill.

The learned Rabbi Arundi of blessed memory wrote in his commentary on Job, in reference to Elihu's initial reply to Job, that it is possible for dreams to contain material that bodes neither good nor ill, as when one dreams of something that has already occurred or of some ordinary mundane event that is a matter of indifference to the dreamer.

With all due respect to the rabbi, however, he does not adequately substantiate this assertion. To begin with, his reference to dreaming of things that have already happened is refuted by our talmudic sages, who have asked, "Is a person ever shown in a dream that which has already occurred?" (*Chullin* 92a). And when he speaks of dreaming of ordinary everyday events, he ignores the fact known to those who are truly versed in the literature of dream interpretation that even these dreams bode either good or ill. This will become clearer to the reader when he understands a principle to be more fully explored in the next gate, namely that the message of a dream is not embodied in its overt literal content but is rather analogous to this content. Thus even a seemingly mundane dream should be interpreted allegorically, as boding either good or ill. This will become plain as the phenomenological purpose of dream communication is revealed, which is essentially what Rabbi Levi ben Gerson deals with in his treatise *Wars of the Lord*. He attributes the existence of dreams to Divine Providence and Guardianship, setting forth that since man has been endowed with free will so that he might choose to seek good and shun evil, and since he has at the same time not been given the foreknowledge of good and evil yet to come, God has provided dreams in compensation for this lack. Man's welfare is thus ultimately in his own hands, for his dreams allow him to make the choice to avoid evil or, by means of repentance, good deeds, prayers, and supplications before the Lord, to reverse His decree. By the same token, when he knows the good that has been foreordained for him, he may intentionally perform such acts as will actualize the acquisition of this good. And thus he may obtain an abundance of good.

Once the purpose of dream communications has been clarified, the wise Arundi's point of view possesses no credence, as the purposeless dreams he speaks of simply do not exist. However, he never accepted the notion of the purposefulness of dreams, for the following reasons. First, if such communication derives from Divine Providence, as we have avowed, it would not be appropriate to find it among the wicked, as in the instances of Pharaoh, Pharaoh's servants, Nebuchadnezzar, and others. Furthermore, even if Arundi had conceded that the dreams of these wicked ones come from the Lord, did it help Pharaoh's servants to avoid being hanged, in the one case, or, in the other, being reinstated? What benefit did they derive from these communications? They were in fact useless! Also, what can one say concerning Nebuchadnezzar, who was powerless to prevent events from unfolding as they did in his dream, despite Daniel's comprehensive interpretation? And what of the dream of Joseph, interpreted in a manner contrary to its true meaning by his father, Jacob, who was not saved thereby from the fulfillment of its prediction that he would bow down before his son? Nor were Pharaoh and all his men of wisdom able to revert the terrible famine that forced the entire nation to sell all of their possessions, their land, and ultimately themselves, although Joseph read Pharaoh's dreams correctly. It may even be that Joseph's solution to the difficulties portrayed by the dream was purely the result of chance. Aside from the fact that all the incidents of Joseph's life until he became Pharaoh's dream interpreter were merely random causes of his reaching that position, note that Joseph's advice to Pharaoh was likewise accidental. Joseph had already finished offering his reading of the dream, and there was no need for him to say anything further. However, since Joseph's intention was to became a prince and leader in the land of Egypt, and since he saw here an opportunity of furthering his ambition, he voluntarily offered his advice to Pharaoh, saying, "Now therefore let Pharaoh look out a man discreet and wise, and set him over the land of Egypt" (Gen. 41:33). Joseph obviously knew that Pharaoh would respond, "Forasmuch as God has shown you all this, there is none so discreet and wise as you" (Gen. 41:39). This concludes the aimless arguments of Arundi!

Every problem he raises, whether general or specific, has more than one solution; these solutions, moreover, are accessible to any intelligent person. I will offer first one response that serves for all the foregoing, then rebut each of his arguments individually. What is immediately obvious to me is that all of the dreams that Arundi presents in contradiction to the thesis of Rabbi Levi ben Gerson were not intended to instruct the dreamer alone, as is usually the case with dreams that come to us from Divine Providence, but were instead special dreams intended to elevate the righteous ones associated with the dreamers. The dreams of Pharaoh's servants were meant to release Joseph from prison and raise his social status, and Nebuchadnezzar's dreams occurred in order to elevate Daniel. Thus the Lord provided that Pharaoh's and Nebuchadnezzar's advisors, be they ever so wise, would read these dreams incorrectly, whereas the interpretations of the righteous ones [Joseph and Daniel] would be fulfilled in their entirety.

Moreover, Providence brings dreams to the righteous and the wicked alike, just as all living things receive their worldly sustenance from the same source. And behold, all people in a state of readiness dream true dreams. This principle is as valid outside the Jewish nation as within, although it is more true among the Jews.

To conclude, when one's dreams foretell evil, he is thereby intended to try to nullify this evil before it comes to pass; and when one dreams of good, he is meant to strive after its fulfillment.

But it is both possible and probable that there will be numerous instances in which the foregoing cannot be accomplished, in which good omens will be voided and evil omens will be fulfilled. Such occurrences are due to the failure of the dreamer either to understand the dream correctly or to perform whatever action the dream required of him.

Be that as it may, I will explain to what extent the endeavors of Joseph's brothers helped to annul the effects of his dream, while at the same time Joseph's actions assisted in the dream's fulfillment. In addition, Joseph's advice to Pharaoh was of benefit to himself as well as to the Egyptians. If not for his interpretation, nothing could have saved them from perishing in the famine, not even their selling their possessions, their land, and finally themselves. But once they knew the dream's interpretation, a practical solution was close at hand, and there is no doubt that Pharaoh's wise men and advisors could have counseled him on their own; yet Joseph came forth with his own counsel. This was a necessity for Joseph and not a matter of his seeking personal gain. Should we accuse him of ulterior motives, we have smuggled the idea from our own minds to avoid shooting ourselves with arrows and awkward questions![12]

Now, although my point requires no further substantiation, I

[12] Almoli's phrase might be translated in modern terms as "we are guilty and full of projections."

will present other supporting arguments from scriptural sources.

As for the notion that one's own efforts are required for the satisfactory outcome of dreams bearing good omens, we may read in the Zohar:

> "And Joseph remembered the dreams which he dreamed" (Gen. 42:9). This is because when a dream contains a good omen, one must not forget it, lest it not be fulfilled. For if such a dream is forgotten by the dreamer, it is likewise forgotten above. Observe that a dream that is not interpreted is like a letter that is not read, for it is as if the dreamer never truly knew the dream. So if a dream is forgotten, it cannot be interpreted, and thus there is no possibility of its fulfillment. Therefore Joseph remembered his dream in order that it would ultimately be fulfilled; he ever retained his faith in its fulfillment. (Gen., *Mikketz* 119b)

This passage states clearly that one must remember one's good dreams in order to strive after their fulfillment. If one forgets these dreams, no effort can be put forth and they will be like unread letters, from which one cannot receive the benefit of what they are meant to communicate. Therefore Joseph held his dream in his memory with great tenacity and exerted all his strength to carry out its message. Jacob, too, placed Joseph's dream in his memory's storehouse: "But his father [Jacob] kept the saying in mind" (Gen. 37:11). The Midrash comments that when Jacob heard Joseph's dream, he took a reed pen and recorded it in detail. Daniel also wrote down his dream as a remembrance until the morning.

We can now see that one should safeguard and remember one's dreams in meticulous detail. According to one's degree of concern, so is his notification. If God sees that the dreamer is unconcerned and attributes no value to his dreams, He will cease to communicate anything essential and will transmit merely insignificant things. Once a dreamer becomes involved with his dreams and seeks to interpret them clearly, however, he should work at fulfilling their messages. Since this work is necessary in dealing with all dreams, and since without this work a dream is virtually meaningless, Joseph was compelled to advise Pharaoh of the means for fulfilling his dream. Thus we read, "Now therefore let Pharaoh . . ." (Gen. 41:33), signifying that offering advice is within the purview of every genuine interpreter, in order for his interpretations to bear fruit. If he fails to give such advice, the dream will not be fulfilled and the interpreter will never know whether his interpretation was true or not.

In conclusion, the purpose of dreaming is as stated by Rabbi Levi ben Gerson: dreams come only with communications of good or evil pertaining to the dreamer.

THE SECOND CHAPTER

It now remains to explicate whether it is possible for dreams to communicate philosophical wisdom.

Rabbi Levi ben Gerson pondered over this very question in *Wars of the Lord*, presenting two arguments that proved conclusively that philosophical ideas cannot be ascertained without their premises, as would be the case with ideas occurring in dreams. If this were not so, then this cognition would be the equivalent of that of God! However, this point of view is not borne out by experience; for instance, men wise in the art of healing have faithfully attested that they have found within the field of medicine many ideas lacking premises. Many such stories have been attributed to Galen.

Rabbi Levi refers to a case in which a person told him of a dream in which he was ordered to take certain medicine for his ailment. The dreamer did not recognize the medicine, however, nor did he know whether it would truly be helpful. He accordingly questioned the physicians, who informed him that the medicine would do him no harm. He subsequently took the medicine and was healed. Also, the rabbi himself, when consciously meditating on deep philosophical matters, would find himself asking about these concerns in his dreams and receiving truthful replies. These were matters on which he had never truly philosophized!

Therefore, "I considered my ways and turned my feet unto Your testimonies" (Ps. 119:59). I believe in full faith that one can acquire valid ideas in the visions of the night, ideas requiring no recourse to proofs and examinations. Yet such ideas are the equivalent of those derived from the philosophical method. This is true in the case of prophecy, where we find that tens of thousands of ideas have come to dreamers who had no prior awareness of the axioms on which these ideas were based, such as the visions of Ezekiel and Isaiah of the chariot (*merkabah*).

A knowledgeable person is always in doubt whether what he has derived as a result of the logical process is in fact true, either because he is not sure if the axioms on which his ideas are based are themselves true or because he must consider the possibility that the conclusions he has drawn from these axioms may not be valid. Such doubts do not affect the prophet or dreamer, however. He does not doubt what he knows and feels confident that what he has been informed about is true, for "God is not a man, that He should lie" (Num. 23:19). It is only because a scholar knows things by means of logic—which is not the case with the prophet or dreamer—that our sages have said, "A scholar is superior to a prophet" (Talmud, *Bava Batra* 12a). But in actuality the reverse is also true.

Accordingly, everything has an answer. When philosophers categorize an idea based on their knowledge of its premises, they rely upon the wisdom of their own time. This idea is true only from the standpoint of its being based on premises that are generally accepted at the time. However, ideas derived from dreams and visions are actually superior, but this phenomenon is not widely known or accepted among scholars—they have never admitted that knowledge derived from dream visions exists! Even if they admitted its existence, they would not consider it to be true knowledge, but merely superficial thought, being that it is not derived from logical premises. But as far as we are concerned, the truth is that this is perfect knowledge and of great benefit.

THE THIRD CHAPTER

The third chapter explains what has been stated by our sages of blessed memory concerning the fact that one perceives in a dream only his own thoughts.

The Talmud states:

> Rabbi Samuel ben Nachmani said in the name of Rabbi Jonathan, "A man is shown in a dream only his own thoughts, for it is said, 'As for you, O King, your thoughts came [into your mind] upon your bed' (Dan. 2:29). Or, similarly, 'That is proven by the fact that a man is never shown in a dream a date palm of gold, or an elephant passing through the eye of a needle' " (*Berakhot* 55b).

I have rethought my own approach and have concluded that this passage includes two explanations: a person is informed of matters that reflect the fact that he has been concerned with them, and he is informed only by means of parables that he has thought about during the day before. So the Talmud offers us a general rule that a dreamer is informed, both by the dream itself and by its interpretation, only of his own thoughts. Thus the Talmud presents two proofs: the scriptural corroboration of the first notion and the experimental corroboration of the second. We must point out, however, that the meaning of the second principle is not that what a person contemplates during the day and subsequently dreams about is necessarily true—an idea that has already been contradicted—but rather that dreams typically concern matters that could actually occur and among which the dreamer's thoughts might meander during the day. I should hasten to add that while these phenomena could occur, they do not in fact occur while one is awake but only in the form of dreaming. Our own experience shows us that we often dream of things we have not thought about during the previous day, yet no one ever dreams of strange things that could never have occurred in waking life. If one ever does have such a dream, it is an exceedingly rare occurrence and comes about only as a result of the dreamer's having laden his mind with very high, very low, or bizarre topics; since we hardly ever concern ourselves with such things, when we do, we are apt to dream about them.

The Fifth Gate

I now will set forth three axioms, revealing the nature of all dreams, that every dream interpreter must know in order for his interpretations to be accurate.

AXIOM 1

A dream that recurs several times in the same guise generally has but one interpretation, which will be fulfilled by but one event. The repetitions occur merely in order for it to be verified and more clearly understood. Occasionally, however, each separate instance of such a dream will be fulfilled by its own discrete event.

If every time this dream recurs it comes to the dreamer in exactly the same mode with no differences whatsoever, or if it recurs bearing the same essential message but employing a different metaphor, it has only one interpretation even if it is repeated a hundred times. If the repetitions occur with precisely the same imagery, the intent is to intensify and lend credence to that which is being communicated; if, on the other hand, the repetitions come with varying imagery, the intent is not merely to strengthen and verify the message but also to ensure that the dreamer understands the imagery, in the event that he failed to understand the first communication. This variation prevents the dream communication from being lost altogether.

AXIOM 2

Aristotle states in his book *De sensu et sensato* that the subject matter of dreams is limited to the dreamer and his personal concerns: his soul and body, his relations, his fellow citizens, and his country. As a rule, one dreams of what is already known, embellished by the dreamer's own imagination. Dreams do not contain concerns that are shared by all of existence collectively, but are relatively limited in their scope.

Our sages have accepted these words of Aristotle as axiomatic but have expanded upon them, stating that this principle applies to the masses of ordinary individuals; but insofar as kings and other rulers are concerned not only with individual but also with collective concerns, their dreams are the dreams of the entire world: " 'Pharaoh dreamed' (Gen. 41:1); but does not everyone dream? This passage shows that the dreams of kings apply to the entire world" (Midrash, *Gen. Rabbah*). The Midrash is saying here that while ordinary people dream of themselves and their individual lives, a king dreams of matters affecting the world; the dream of the king is as it were the dream of all his people, coming to him because of his collective role in society. Rabbi Isaac concurs:

> Although it has been affirmed that no one is shown anything in a dream save that which is appropriate to his own spiritual level, it is otherwise with kings, who are permitted to see more deeply than others; for inasmuch as a king's level of spirituality is more elevated than that of ordinary persons, he is permitted to see that which is pertinent to that level. Thus Scripture states that "what God is about to do He hath declared unto Pharaoh" (Gen. 41:25), whereas to other men God does not reveal what He is about to do, unless they be prophets, saints, or sages. (Zohar, Gen., *Mikketz* 194b)

AXIOM 3

We must bear in mind that in dreams we do not see exactly what is to occur, so that it is then fulfilled, but rather dreams communicate using metaphor or allegory as a vehicle. This applies to prophecy as well. We may observe that all of the dreams recorded in Scripture came to the dreamers in this fashion.

THE SIXTH GATE

The sixth gate will discuss the fact that one should interpret a dream based on the dreamer's vocation and other circumstances.

It is well known to any person who is wise of heart that although two people may dream the same dream, the interpretation may be quite different for each dreamer. For example, the motif of a horse appearing in a dream will sometimes indicate wisdom and at other times physical strength. If a scholar dreams of a river that seems difficult to cross, which he nevertheless is able to cross through the effort and power of his horse, his dream should read as showing that by means of his wisdom he will be able to accomplish things that would otherwise be impossible. But should the dreamer not be a scholar, the dream would refer to actual physical prowess. To take another instance, for an armed robber to dream of being hanged from a palm tree would not carry the same meaning as the identical dream dreamed by a rabbinical scholar. Each dreamer is to derive a unique interpretation dependent upon his own activities and mode of life. For the robber the interpretation is that he will literally be hanged from the gallows, whereas for the scholar the dream connotes elevation and authority.

This idea is corroborated in the Talmud:

> Rabbi Chanina had seen in a dream that Rab was being hanged from the branch of a palm tree, and since traditionally such a dream is interpreted to mean that he who is thus hanged will become a leader, the rabbi concluded that Rab would be raised to a position of authority. (*Yoma* 87b)

The foregoing text appears as a self-evident rabbinical truth, but such insight is obscured from the view of those fools who glorify themselves in the science of dream interpretation and yet know nothing about it.

The Seventh Gate

The following investigation will be extremely beneficial in that it will resolve the question of whether dreams actually coincide with their interpretation.

THE FIRST CHAPTER

THE INVESTIGATION AND INQUIRIES

Behold these words from the Talmud: "A dream that is not interpreted is like a letter that is not read." This passage could be expounded upon to mean that if a dream is not interpreted, as when one is silent and does not reveal his dream (so that it cannot be interpreted), it is as if the dream were never dreamed. It will not be fulfilled in any way, neither for good nor for ill, just as when a letter arrives from afar and sits unopened and unread, it is as if the letter had never been sent, for the recipient has no knowledge of its contents. It is also stated that "all dreams follow the mouth," the usual reading being that the interpretation of a dream affects its actual outcome, as when "it came to pass as he [Joseph] interpreted to us" (Gen. 41:13). In other words, if a dream indicates evil but is given a positive interpretation, it will in fact be fulfilled by good circumstances and not evil, and vice versa. It has also been stated:

> There were twenty-four interpreters of dreams in Jerusalem. Once I dreamed a dream and consulted all of them, receiving a different interpretation from each—and all were fulfilled, thus

confirming that "all dreams follow the mouth." Is this quotation scriptural? According to Rabbi Eleazar it is: "How do we know that all dreams follow the mouth? Because it says, 'And it came to pass as he interpreted to us' " (Talmud, *Berakhot* 55b)

Thus, according to this interpretation, one could ask, "When are the interpretations that have been set down in the Talmud and in dream books fulfilled?" There is nothing to prevent the dreamer from remaining quiet and not relating his dream to anyone, so that it could not be interpreted for him. It is likewise possible that he might tell the dream to someone and that it would be interpreted differently from the readings given in the Talmud and in dream books. In the former case, it is as if his dream had never occurred and thereby becomes totally insignificant, but if it is interpreted for him, it will be fulfilled according to the interpretation as given, not according to the books! This being the situation, the efforts of wise men to set down the interpretations of dreams was a futile endeavor, since when we follow the interpretations of others, the dream's outcome will be given, and if the dream is not interpreted at all, it will never come to pass.

With further research, however, we can see that this is not truly the case. The wise men of the past did not write only of comforting omens, so that a person consulting a dream book would find only consolation for his soul; were this so, everyone's dreams would be good, without exception. So we are still left with a dilemma. We might consider that if dreams follow the interpreters' mouths, and one could thereby cancel the interpretations to be found in the books, then any fool could set himself up as an interpreter, as wisdom would no longer be a prerequisite for practicing this profession! But this is assuredly not true, for there is unquestionably great wisdom here. As Pharaoh said to Joseph, "Forasmuch as God has shown you all this, there is none so discreet and wise as you." It is also stated in the Scripture, concerning Daniel, whose wisdom greatly exceeded that of his peers, in that he knew far more of the interpretation of dreams, "Now as for these four youths, God gave them knowledge and skill in all learning and wisdom; and Daniel had understanding in all visions and dreams" (Dan. 1:17). It seems that the possessor of such wisdom was thought of as being very elevated, since Daniel alone was worthy of being given it.

Therefore, dream interpretation is dependent upon wisdom, and not anyone who takes upon himself the title of dream interpreter is entitled to it, but only one in a city or two in a family. We see that Joseph said, "Do not interpretations belong to God?" He also said, "It is not in me; God will give Pharaoh an answer of peace" (Gen. 41:16). We can understand from these words of Joseph's that the interpretation of dreams is within the realm of the divine; only one who possesses the spirit of God will grasp its truth.

So it would seem that the statement "All dreams follow the mouth" means precisely the opposite of what it appears to say, insofar as it is applied to any and all interpreters, regardless of their level of expertise. What is even more bizarre and problematic is that since we have assumed that what God ordains for the future He tells to whomever He chooses, showing the person what will happen to him in the future by means of a visionary dream, it is theoretically possible that when dreams remain uninterpreted, God's communications would be voided, and when dreams are interpreted, God's communications could be altered according to the will of the interpreter! It is also difficult to accept the notion that all dreams follow our mouths, considering what our sages have set down in the Midrash concerning "There was none that could interpret them unto Pharaoh" (Gen. 41:8):

> There were indeed interpretations of the dream, but these interpretations were unacceptable to him. For example, the seven well-favored and fat-fleshed kine mean that you will beget seven daughters, the seven ill-favored and lean-fleshed kine

> that you will bury seven daughters, the seven full ears of corn that you will conquer seven provinces, and the seven thin ears that seven provinces will revolt against you. (Midrash, *Gen. Rabbah, Mikketz* 89:6)

But we never find in the biblical narrative that these interpretations were fulfilled, for the very reason that they were untrue. So, too, are the numerous dreams that a person may have interpreted that are never fulfilled as interpreted. We cannot merely say that this mistakenly interpreted dream is annulled and therefore has no interpretation, because we have established the principle that "there is no dream without its interpretation." Thus we must ascertain in what sense we are to understand "All dreams follow the mouth."

We should also ask how it is possible for a dream to be interpreted by one person in one way and by another in the opposite way. If there is any science here, it should possess a unified wisdom, so that what one finds to be true, the other should also find to be true. It seems that the Tosafists [annotators of the Talmud] addressed this very question, in their commentary on the talmudic passage concerning the twenty-four dream interpreters:

> It seems to Rabbi Isaac that it is the stellar configuration rising at the time of birth of the interpreter that brings about his interpretive ability and that it is not dependent upon wisdom. (*Berakhot* 55b)

But to my way of thinking this proposal is an insufficient explanation, as long as I can observe that in our age "there [is] no frequent vision" (1 Sam. 3:1), and as long as I have discovered not one person whose dream interpretations have all been fulfilled! If this vocation were dependent upon astrology, it would seem likely that even in this day and age we would find some person all of whose interpretations are fulfilled, as in the days of old.

THE SECOND CHAPTER

A clarification of three propositions that are needed to resolve this dilemma.

PROPOSITION 1

One should always bear in mind that the rules governing dream interpretation must be based in part upon a prior detailed knowledge of the dreamer's individual circumstances. The process of divining the future of the dreamer thus involves not only the interpreter's skill but also his special knowledge of the dreamer's life, with all its implications. And, in addition, what the interpreter has conjectured should be consistent with the allusions presented by the dream. The ability to accomplish this is given only to persons destined to provide advice and assistance to others, to enlighten the ignorant. Behold that the person who possesses this intuitive power brings together past, present, and future so that they coincide with the suggestions embodied by the dream. He must furthermore have the intellectual capacity to comprehend allegory, and the often enigmatic words of the sages of the past, and bring this power to bear on his reading of the dream's teachings.

In the case of Joseph the Righteous, his powers of intuition were strengthened by his expertise in matters of business and in the acquisition of wealth through speculation, knowing infallibly which commodities would rise in value and which would decline. King Solomon of blessed memory had this to say concerning such ability: "The hand of the diligent makes rich" (Prov. 10:4). By this measure Joseph was a phenomenon. Potiphar and his wife observed Joseph's great fortune in all of his undertakings, in the home and in the field. His superiority in the art of intuition is also evident in the advice he gave to Pharaoh, whereby Pharaoh acquired all of the wealth of the entire land of Egypt. With this power Joseph likewise accurately read the dreams of Pharaoh's servants, which could quite plausibly have been interpreted as having the same reading, for the Scripture states, "And they dreamed a dream of both of them" (Gen. 40:5). Joseph nonetheless gave each his separate interpretation based upon what he knew of them previously from spending time in their company, as well as what he knew of the differences in their professions and their relative closeness to the king. Joseph knew that the butler was closer to the king than the baker, since the butler was always in the presence of Pharaoh when the latter was drinking, while the baker never entered there. Joseph also knew the difference between the offenses for which they had been arrested. These facts were surely known to him, for it is impossible that Joseph, having been imprisoned with them, would not have questioned them on these matters and learned all they had to tell. Consider the words of our rabbis of blessed memory:

> A fly was found in the goblet of wine prepared for Pharaoh by the butler, and a pebble in the cake prepared by the baker. This is why it is said, "The butler of the king of Egypt and his baker offended their lord" (Gen. 40:1), implying that they had failed in the duties they performed for Pharaoh. (Midrash, Gen. *Rabbah, Vayeshev* 88:2)

Therefore Joseph intuited the punishment that the servants' offenses would incur. In the case of the butler, where a fly was discovered in Pharaoh's goblet, he should have been forgiven, as it could not have been in his power to prevent such a mishap from occurring. What could he have done? The fly fell into the goblet all on its own! Joseph therefore pronounced that the butler should be restored to his former position. But in the case of the baker, where a pebble was discovered in Pharaoh's cake, this was clearly due to the negligence of the baker, who should have been more attentive to his professional duties. Joseph thus pronounced that the baker would end up on the gallows. The "three days" within which Joseph predicted the dreams would be fulfilled was plausible, in that he knew that three days remained until Pharaoh's birthday, at which time it was customary to call forth all the workers and give them presents and money, as well as to bring up all the prisoners from the dungeon and decree who was to live and who was to die. So Joseph, with his knowledge of all these pertinent factors, was capable of recognizing the difference between the two dreams, although they seemed to refer to quite similar circumstances. Thus it is with all genuine and wise interpreters.

PROPOSITION 2

It must be borne in mind that every dream contains numerous and differing indications, for evil and for good, on a multiplicity of topics. This is what Joseph was alluding to when he said to Pharaoh, "Do not interpretations belong to God?" He intentionally used the plural, *interpretations,* for Joseph interpreted both for contemporary and for future generations, as we know from the words of our rabbis of blessed memory in the Midrash.

I believe that King Solomon was also referring to this notion when he stated that "a dream comes through multitude of business." In other words, dreams have a multifarious character and do not arrive to bring only a single communication or to deal with only one of the dreamer's concerns. So we find that Joseph's brothers interpreted Joseph's dreams in two different ways: " 'Shall you indeed reign over us? or shall you indeed have dominion over us?' " (Gen. 37:8). The question was, would Joseph rule over his brothers, or was his rulership over them in the dream a symbol for his ruling others? As it transpired, both interpretations were fulfilled, for Joseph ruled over the land of Egypt as well as over his brothers.

PROPOSITION 3

It is virtually impossible to find a genuine interpreter, one who is both learned and wise, who possesses the capacity to comprehend every one of a dream's implications and to read them with total objectivity and infallibility. Some errors are unavoidable. One should therefore never rely merely on his own interpretations but should seek out a learned interpreter and be guided by him, as I have discussed previously.

THE THIRD CHAPTER

It should by now be evident that the meaning of our sages' words "All dreams follow the mouth" was not that an interpreter could nullify a dream communication by offering a reading that opposes the dream's true teaching; this saying can surely be explained by one of the three foregoing propositions.

The first explanation corresponds to the first proposition: that the meaning of the dream is to be derived mainly from the interpreter's subsequent interrogation of the dreamer. He should question the dreamer closely regarding that person's particular circumstances before applying his intuitive powers to formulate his interpretation. The word *mouth* is to be understood in the same context as the words of our Lord [to Moses]: "Who has made man's mouth? I will be with your mouth, and teach you what you shall speak" (Exod. 4:11–12).

The second explanation is that since all dreams bear multiple communications, the interpreter—however expert he may be—cannot possibly understand everything a dream has to say; he can only interpret part of a dream and must leave the rest unread or even unnoticed. Thus the dreamer will be attentive only to the fragments of the dream that have been interpreted for him. When this interpretation is fulfilled, he will recognize it as such. The other aspects of the dream will also be fulfilled, but without the dreamer's being aware of the fact. Had he sought out a different interpreter, this person would likely have interpreted another part of the dream, with the result that the dreamer would have focused on that communication instead. Thus, however the dream is interpreted, it will still "follow the mouth." What remains undiscovered and thereby uninterpreted in a dream, although it too is ultimately fulfilled, means nothing to the dreamer who is ignorant of both its existence and its import. The foregoing also explains the existence of the twenty-four dream interpreters, for each of them would recognize a different feature of the same dream.

The third explanation is based on the third proposition. "Lean not upon your own understanding. . . . Be not wise in your own eyes" (Prov. 3:5, 7). That is to say, do not interpret your own dreams as the spirit moves you. A dream can speak to you only after it has been interpreted; without this interpretation a dream is nothing, as if it had never been dreamed. Recall that "a dream that is not interpreted is like a letter that is not read." So, to paraphrase the saying, "all dreams follow their interpretations," for dream communications are given to humanity with the understanding that they will be interpreted.

This also clarifies further the notion that a dream that is not interpreted is like a letter that is not read. The significance of this statement is not that if the dreamer remains silent the dream will not be fulfilled; the dream will be fulfilled regardless, but without the dreamer's awareness of the fact. This is further discussed in the Zohar:

> Rabbi Chiya and Rabbi Jose formerly studied with Rabbi Simeon. Rabbi Chiya once put to Rabbi Simeon this question: "We have learned that a dream that is not interpreted is like a letter that is not read. Does this mean that the dream comes true without the dreamer being conscious of the fact, or does it mean that it remains unfulfilled?" Rabbi Simeon answered, "The dream comes true but without the dreamer being aware of it." (Gen., *Vayeshev* 183b)

This can likewise be confirmed by the analogy to a letter that is not read. Just as a letter arriving from a distant place was sent to notify the recipient of something that could mean either harm or benefit to him, if he does not open it, or even if he reads it and fails to understand it, he will not be able to prepare for the harm or benefit that the letter might portend. Yet no one would imagine that the contents of the letter will remain unfulfilled merely because of the ignorance of the recipient. Fulfillment there will be, but he will not be conscious of this. This is exactly parallel to the situation with dreams.

We may conclude that the dictum of our sages of blessed memory to the effect that "all dreams follow the mouth" was not intended to convey the idea that a dream interpreter can randomly alter the meaning of a dream. Rabbah, writing in the Talmud, adds to this statement the following: "This is true only if the interpretation corresponds to the content of the dream" (*Berakhot* 55b). In other words, the interpretation must fit the dream, pointing at what the Master of Dreams intended. But if the interpreter reads what is brought to him in an untruthful manner, there is no question but that the dream will still be fulfilled. Therefore, the interpretations that Pharaoh's advisors derived from his dream were not fulfilled.

The precepts of dream interpretation that are laid down in the Talmud and in other books that deal with the subject are thus general rules. By employing the notions laid forth in this book, and by applying knowledge, rational powers, and intuition, an interpreter will be able to discern and read clearly the multiple communications of all dreams. To be sure, there is esoteric knowledge that will never be found in books, yet this is nevertheless accessible to all true interpreters.

Bar Hedya, for instance, was both expert and wise in the science of dream interpretation; the Talmud introduces him by saying, "Bar Hedya was an interpreter of dreams" (*Berakhot* 56a), showing all that this was his profession. He had the capacity to recognize every one of the communications contained within a dream, as well as the pertinent details of the dreamer's circumstances. Therefore, when a dreamer paid him his fee, he would report all the good omens portrayed in the dream and omit all the omens of foreboding, however many there might be. But for those dreamers who did not pay his fee, he would do just the opposite, interpreting for his client the predictions of ill and leaving out the good omens.[13] This was a device to raise his prices, for those who sought him out inferred that good interpretations depended on how much they spent. Also, Bar Hedya recognized that Rabbah had an afflicted birth chart, as it was Rabbah who stated that "people and their sustenance are dependent not upon their personal merit but only upon the constellation under which they were born." Bar Hedya sensed that Rabbah held this view only because it was in fact his own situation. He then interpreted Rabbah's dream based on this insight: " 'The letter *vav* of the word *chamor* [donkey] has been erased from your phylacteries.'[14] Rabbah looked, and indeed the letter *vav* was no longer there" (*Berakhot* 56a). It could not be said that this occurred as a result of the interpretation. Furthermore, he could not have interpreted for Abaye in this way even if he had not paid him his fee, for in reality this did not exist, an interpreter not being a magician! This being the case, since Bar Hedya was compelled to derive his interpretation from the actual facts of the situation, why was Rabbah so enraged with him? And why did Bar Hedya consider himself to be a sinner, necessarily fearing Rabbah's curse? It seems that the law was in Rabbah's favor! A considered response might be that Rabbah was unfamiliar with the science of dream interpretation and so was unaware of Bar Hedya's device of suiting his interpretation to the fee he was paid, thinking naively that a dream may be interpreted in a single way and refers to only one concern. It is said that Rabbah did not know the principle that "all dreams follow the mouth," considering the fact that when he read these words in Bar Hedya's dream book, he understood them only in the most simplistic sense and thus became very angry with Bar Hedya. However, the latter was unwilling to reveal

[13] See page 103 for an excerpt from the story of Bar Hedya.

[14] Phylacteries (*tefillin*) are small leather cases that Jewish men wear on the head and arm during the morning prayer. Inside the cases are parchments inscribed with passages from the Torah, including one that refers to a *chamor*, or donkey (Exod. 13:13). The obliteration of one of the letters on the parchment would render it invalid for ritual use.

the meaning of this saying to Rabbah. Rabbah was also angered because Bar Hedya could have interpreted his dreams in a way that he would not have found so baffling and that would not have accelerated him on the path toward the evil that lay in wait for him. But Bar Heyda did not interpret the dreams with such clarity and thoroughness but related to Rabbah their portents of evil as if he were an enemy in revenge, for Rabbah did not pay him his fee. This view is supported by Rabbah's having said to Bar Hedya, "You gave me all this pain." Apparently what Bar Hedya offered Rabbah via his interpretation was only pain, and it was for this that he punished himself with exile.

In this manner we can explain what is found in the Midrash Rabbah and other *midrashim*:

> A certain woman went to Rabbi Eleazar and said to him, "I saw in a dream that the loft of the upper story of my house was split open." "You will conceive a son," replied the rabbi. She went away and it happened just as he had told her. Later she dreamed the same dream again, and again came to Rabbi Eleazar and told him of it, and he gave her the same interpretation, which was fulfilled just as it had been the first time. She then had this dream a third time and again sought out the rabbi. She did not find him, however, and so she told his disciples, "I saw in a dream that the loft of the upper story of my house was split open." "You will bury your husband," replied the disciples. She went away, and it happened just as they had told her. Rabbi Eleazar, upon hearing weeping and wailing, asked what had occurred, and the disciples related it to him. "You have murdered the man!" he said to them, reprimanding them with the passage from Genesis (41:13) to the effect that "it came to pass as he interpreted it to us." (*Gen. Rabbah, Mikketz* 89:8)

When the rabbi said, "You have murdered the man," he was saying that they should not have announced this evil so baldly. For then the woman knew that her husband, who was ill, would not survive his illness, and therefore did not exert much effort to save him, as she surely would have done had she believed there was a chance that he might yet live. And this neglect could have been the very reason he died. From this point of view, it is certainly as if the disciples murdered the man. Furthermore, when the husband learned of his imminent demise, surely he lost his will to live, and this in itself could have hastened his death. It would have been more appropriate for the disciples to have told the woman, "This is what the dream predicts, but you must go to God and beseech Him to remove this evil from you." The simple statement that her husband would die permitted the woman to think that this decree was already written and sealed with the ring of the Lord and therefore could not be reversed.

With this in mind, I propose that when a person comes seeking an interpretation of a dream, it is proper to tell him or her the truth, however it may appear to the interpreter. If it is a portent of foreboding, he should tell the dreamer to strive to alter this dire progression of events and to seek mercy; if it is good news, he should urge him to strive to attain its fulfillment. This concept came to me only after deep and thorough research and cogitation, and is corroborated by comments found in the twenty-ninth gate of the book *Akedat Yitzchak* ("The Binding of Isaac") by Rabbi Isaac Arama[15] of blessed memory. However, I then came across a contrary notion in the Zohar:

> "And Joseph dreamed a dream, and he told it to his brethren; and they hated him yet more" (Gen. 37:5). From this we should take heed that one should tell his dreams only to someone who is his close friend. Otherwise the listener might pervert the significance of the dream and bring about a delay in its fulfillment. The fact that Joseph told his dream to his brothers caused its fulfillment to be delayed for twenty-two years. (Gen., *Vayeshev* 183a)

It seems inescapable, then, that an interpreter does have the power to misinterpret a dream in accordance with his own desires and in utter opposition to the dream's true meaning.

[15] A Spanish rabbi of the fifteenth century.

On the other hand, with more insight into this passage we can see that it actually agrees with all that precedes it. This becomes evident when we apprehend the purpose of dream communications: namely, that dreams come to us as a result of God's providence and guardianship. Knowing this, we should be able to reason that if one has a dream indicating that some good is coming to him, and if he then asks his enemy to interpret the dream, the enemy will be inclined to interpret the dream perversely, as alluding to some forthcoming evil. He will not be likely to wish to tell the dreamer the truth. Consequently, the dreamer, having no awareness of the good that has been foretold, will not put forth the necessary effort to achieve its actualization and will never attain it. And even if he were to attain it, he would not receive the abundance of good that would have been his portion had he promoted his own fortune by working in concert with the images of the dream. Not only this, but since he will consider the evil interpretation offered by his enemy to be true, he will attempt to avert this evil outcome—which effort will of course be pointless—and this behavior in itself constitutes illness. But when one tells his dream to someone who loves him, the friend will assuredly interpret the truth for him—whether for good or for ill—so that the dreamer will strive either to draw near to the good or to separate himself from the ill.

Thus the Zohar states that one should tell his dream only to someone who is his close friend, for if he tells his enemy, it will be transformed into something other than what was intended. It could even come about, if the dream portended good and the dreamer was informed otherwise, it would be changed into evil as a result of the dreamer's unnecessary efforts to fulfill a misinterpretation. There is no doubt that one's enemy would try to prevent a good outcome from occurring. This is the significance of the Zohar's reference to Joseph, who related his dream to his brothers and thereby delayed its fulfillment for twenty-two years.

The Eighth Gate

Herein follows an explication of the signs by which one may know whether a dream will be fulfilled quickly or be delayed.

First, when a dreamer sees his dream very clearly, as if he were actually awake, with the result that when he awakens he recalls every detail without the slightest omission, this is to be taken as a sign that the dream will be quickly fulfilled. But if the dream is vague, so that he remembers little upon awakening, just to the degree that it seems unreal to him will the dream be delayed in its fulfillment. By the same token, should he remember part and forget part, the dream will be fulfilled neither at once nor in the distant future, but somewhere between these extremes, the time between the dream and its fulfillment depending upon its degree of clarity to the dreamer.

Another test, set forth by a man of wisdom, consists in observing how long before daybreak the dream occurs. The nearer to morning, the sooner the time of the dream's fulfillment. He considered each hour as corresponding to a month, so that if one has a dream there hours prior to dawn, it will be fulfilled within three months, and so on. This has been verified by the Midrash:

> Rabbi Jochanan said that any dream that occurs close to the morning will arrive at its outcome very soon. *Gen. Rabbah, Mikketz* 89:5)

Therefore, in the case of Pharaoh, when his dream occurred close to dawn, it was quickly fulfilled, while the dream of Nebuchadnezzar, occurring during the night, was delayed in its fulfillment.

Finally and most significantly, one must always take note of the nature of the material appearing in the dream and then relate it to the dreamer's own life, in order to determine whether it is plausible that the dream might be fulfilled soon. This test requires the interpreter's intuitive power. We should recall how Joseph was able to determine that the dreams of Pharaoh's servants would be fulfilled within three days, since Joseph was aware that Pharaoh's birthday was three days hence. Also, in regard to Joseph's own dreams (Gen. 37), one might have expected their interpreters to realize—from the nature of the dreams' content—that they could hardly be fulfilled in the immediate future, but only when the circumstances and the people involved were disposed appropriately for such fulfillment.

This completes the eighth gate alongside the other gates.
Thank the Lord!

3. The Dream as Personal Prophecy

What are dreams and where do they come from? What kinds of messages do they give us, and what areas of our lives are they concerned with? Every dream theorist seeks to formulate some general principles to encompass the nature and purpose of dreams, and every system of dream interpretation arises within a particular culture with its own beliefs and values. Before going more specifically into the Jewish view of dreams as exemplified by Almoli, let's look briefly at the ideas of the two great modern dream theorists, Freud and Jung.

For both Freud and Jung, dream theory evolved out of their practice of clinical psychiatry and the needs of their patients. Freud saw the dream as a psychological mechanism that served to keep the dreamer asleep by expressing, in disguised form, the repressed feelings and desires buried in the unconscious. Most of Freud's patients were suffering from a neurosis called hysteria, which Freud saw as resulting from the repression of some traumatic early experience, usually of a sexual nature, that was too terrible for the patient to accept consciously. The goal of treatment was to bring this repressed material to the surface. The dream, as the royal road to the unconscious, was the tool for gaining access to these buried feelings, through the technique of free association.

Jung's ideas—and his differences with Freud—were strongly influenced by his philosophical outlook. The son of a Protestant minister, Jung felt that the challenge of life was to achieve a meaningful and fulfilling existence, and he regarded this task as a psychological phenomenon that could be separated from conventional Christianity and other institutional creeds and churches. He thus saw himself as guiding his patients in areas that were formerly the domain of religion. Jung formulated his own psychological constructs, such as the complexes and archetypes, and developed notions such as that of individuation, the process of attaining a wholeness and balance of the psyche and the fulfillment of one's unique individuality. Dreams play a central role in the process of individuation, for they are seen as the voice of the unconscious, which consists of numerous complexes and the organizing principles that Jung called the Self. Jung essentially combined religion and psychoanalysis by substituting "the unconscious" or "the Self" for what religion called "God." The dream was elevated to a lofty position of spokesperson for this unconscious seat of wisdom.

In Almoli's view, dreams are symbolic messages from God to help individuals navigate their way through the complexities of their personal destiny. (Although we are switching back to "God" instead of "the unconscious" or "the Self," we now have a picture of dreams that is similar to Jung's.) The dream is seen as part of the system of checks and balances that God introduced into His creation in order that people might lead righteous lives. Thus, a dream is either a reflection that we are on the right track and would benefit from pursuing our current direction, or it is a warning that we are missing the mark and must repent so as to avert the evil decree. This view is consistent with the traditional folk belief in dreams as omens, except that Almoli expands or elevates the notion, allowing the dream to play a part in the acquisition of knowledge. The dream is a divine gift to mankind and a blessing for those who understand its message.

It is important to distinguish between the "bad" dream that is a warning from God to change one's course and the "bad" or false dream that comes from demonic sources. Judaism posits the existence of two inclinations in the soul: the *yetzer ha-tov*, or good inclination, which inclines us in the direction of the righteous life, and the *yetzer ha-rah*, or evil inclination, which motivates us toward wickedness. A continuous conflict is assumed to exist within each person as to which inclination to follow. The Jews have been wary of the possibility that dreams might fall into the hands of the evil inclination. A Chasidic rabbi once explained to me why he gives no value to dreams. Since the Talmud says that a dream can come from either an angel or a demon, this rabbi rationalized that he was better off ignoring all dreams, as he felt unsure of his ability to identify the source of a dream. But for Almoli, who believed that God reserved the ordinary dream to communicate His will to mankind, the demonic dream was more the exception than the rule. The rule was that dreams usually come from God and reflect His benevolent concern for human beings.

Gabriel: The Master of Dreams

Almoli's assertion that dreams come from God is not very specific. We might ask precisely which aspect of God sends us dreams. Is it Yahweh, Elohim, Adonai, the Shekhinah, one of the Ten Sefirot? Almoli refers to the source of dreams by a few epithets, such as the Master of Dreams and the Spinner of Dreams. The Talmud says that the Master of Dreams is an angel, but far as I know it does not state which angel plays this role.[1] Several mystical treatises, however—notably the Zohar—identify Gabriel as the Master of Dreams.

When I first noticed this fact, I had one of those intuitive flashes that convinced me of the appropriateness of the appointment. I realized that the name Gabriel in Hebrew—a composite of the words for "man" (*gever*) and "God" (*El*)—symbolizes humanity's lifelong search for communion with God and for an understanding of the divine forces operating in human life. To achieve this understanding through a study of dreams would depend on the capacity to connect the human and divine realms in some meaningful way. As the connecting link between the two, Gabriel brings man to God and God to man, thus divinizing man and humanizing God. The dream is a manifestation of God in search of humanity and of our human need to recognize our own innate divine powers.

Gabriel appears in various places throughout Jewish literature.

By looking at his attributes and activities, we can gain some sense of the potential role of dreams in the drama of our lives.

Instructor of the Soul. The Zohar identifies Gabriel as the angel who, as mentioned in numerous legends and *midrashim*, instructs the soul before its birth. Not only does the fetus *in utero* learn "all the Torah from beginning to end,"[2] but it also learns the "seventy languages of the world."[3] The connection of Gabriel with dreams suggests that the dream is a carrier of the *a priori* experience of the soul.[4] Symbolically, Gabriel embodies the possibility that dreams can bring us into contact with the world of the soul's origin—what Jung referred to as the archetypal realm—connecting us to our spiritual and ancestral roots and to the soul's vast storehouse of wisdom. Dreams are the bridge that can assist in the creative union between our conscious and unconscious life.

Observer and Judge. Again in the Zohar, Gabriel is the representation of the good inclination, the voice of conscience. Closely related to this function is Gabriel's work of observing and recording the deeds of human beings. In a mystical legend of the great sixteenth-century Kabbalist Isaac Luria, Gabriel is pictured as wielding the stylus of a scribe. In another legend, he has the writing materials of a scribe girded around his waist, in order to observe and record people's concerns, plans, and actions, both the good and the bad.[5] This information is then presented to God. We might speculate that the dream is God's feedback to us based upon Gabriel's report on our activities.

Both judgment and justice are associated with Gabriel. The word *gever*, the part of Gabriel's name that I translated as "man," is also related to the word for strength, *gevurah*. As one of the Ten Sefirot of the kabbalistic Tree of Life, *gevurah* is often translated as "judgment." Girded with his sword of justice, Gabriel is the protector of the innocent in several legends.[6]

The Jewish Hermes? As a messenger of God, Gabriel has much in common with the Greek god Hermes, who also plays the role of mediating between the conscious and unconscious and hence is associated with dreams. Hermes brings fire to mankind (symbolically, enlightenment or inspiration), and Gabriel is the prince of fire.[7] Both have the attribute of moving swiftly[8] and are able to change form when necessary, connecting them symbolically with the power of transmutation or transformation. Both are associated with death; Hermes conducts souls to the underworld, and Gabriel acts as a messenger of death, along with the angels Sammael and Metatron.[9] At the same time, Gabriel, like Hermes, is associated with healing. For instance, Gabriel is one of the angels who visits Abraham when he is recovering from his circumcision.[10]

Hermes represents the power of the spoken word, and Gabriel too is connected to understanding the word, as when he commands Daniel, "Look into the word and understand the vision" (Dan. 9:23). Although dreams are primarily visual images, we record or describe our dreams in words, on which the interpretation of the dreams is based. Also, many dreams utilize words themselves as images.

Especially interesting is the attribute of playful deception shared by Gabriel and Hermes—a characteristic of what Jungians call the trickster archetype. Like Hermes, the sweet-talking liar and thief, Gabriel has a habit of trickery. According to one legend, the child Moses enraged the Pharaoh one day by seizing the crown from his head and placing it on his own head.[11] Pharaoh called his counselors and wise men to give their opinions on how to deal with the child. Many of them advised that Moses should be put to death as a threat to the safety of the realm, since clearly he acted with deliberation and purpose. God then sent His angel Gabriel, who took the form of a wise old man (an example of Gabriel as the shape-shifter) and suggested that a test be made to see whether Moses truly was wise enough to have acted deliberately. Accordingly, two pots were brought, one filled with gold and the other with live coals. If Moses were to reach for the gold, this would indicate wisdom beyond his years and hence his guilt. If he grasped the coals, it would be clear that he was devoid of reason and innocent. When the bowls were placed before Moses, he began to stretch out his hand for the gold. Just in time,

Gabriel, who had become invisible, caught the child's hand and directed it toward the coals, thus saving the life of Israel's redeemer. If the choice is between deception and losing a life, Gabriel represents the need to lie and trick, or what might be called the principle of positive deception. Another example of such creative deception is the role that Rebecca played in tricking Isaac into blessing Jacob instead of Esau in Genesis 27.

The trickster element in dreams is also suggested by a kabbalistic idea, cited by Almoli, that during sleep the soul rises up to heaven and amuses itself with God. In other Jewish legends, the soul is said to leave the sleeping body and wander over the face of the earth, reporting back its experiences to the sleepless mind.[12] In the Midrash, "During sleep the soul departs and draws spiritual refreshment from on high."[13] In all of these examples, sleep is portrayed not as a passive withdrawal but as an active experience for the soul.

The notion of the soul amusing itself with God adds a further insight: dreaming is playing. Dreams tell a story and both Gabriel and Hermes often communicate through the language of stories, or parables. Like the trickster storyteller of Greek myth, Gabriel brings fantasies and stories to the sleeper. Laughter is an important factor here, as when Hermes is caught lying by a god and quickly tells a story to make the god laugh and distract him. Perhaps our unconscious laughs at our dream stories, not only to amuse itself but also for the healing effect of laughter and to preserve our sense of humor.

Dream Interpreter. Gabriel makes his appearance in the Book of Daniel in the role of dream interpreter:

> And while I was speaking, and praying, and confessing my sin and the sin of my people Israel, and presenting my supplications before the Lord my God for the holy mountain of my God; yea, while I was speaking in prayer, the man Gabriel, whom I had seen in the vision at the beginning, being caused to fly swiftly, approached close to me about the time of the evening offering. And he made me to understand, and talked with me, and said: "O Daniel, I am now come forth to make

you skillful of understanding. At the beginning of your supplications a word went forth, and I am come to declare it; for you are greatly beloved: therefore look into the word and understand the vision. Seventy weeks are decreed upon your people and upon the holy city, to finish your transgression, and to make an end of sin, and to forgive iniquity, and to bring in everlasting righteousness." (Dan. 9:20–25)

In this passage, we find Gabriel empowered with the quality of understanding, or *binah*. Gabriel's role, like that of all dream interpreters, is to facilitate understanding through dream material. As one of the Ten Sefirot in Kabbalah, *binah*, the quality of receptive intelligence, is considered to be feminine; in fact, this *sefirah* is known as the Mother.

A key note here is the connection of the dream to the future. Whether for a group or an individual, dreams are a form of prophecy, which focuses on the future dimension. While it is evident that dreams utilize the past as a source of images, the actual purpose of most dreams is to facilitate a creative union between the past and present, while laying the foundation for future possibilities. This is clearly the case in dreams throughout the Bible, where God communicates to people through their "visions of the night" about present and future concerns. Angels like Gabriel represent the whisperings of our mind that we commonly refer to as intuition. Intuitions can come to us through dreamwork, and it is the task of the dream interpreter to help uncover these hidden meanings and allusions.

Above all else, the interpretation of dreams requires a strong intuitive mind—what the Book of Daniel calls the capacity to understand "the handwriting on the wall." Whereas traditional Judaism emphasizes intellectual study and the masculine value of analytical thought, the art of dream interpretation calls on the feminine, intuitive powers of the soul. It is unfortunate that religious Jews today rarely acknowledge the value of dreams and intuitions; if they did, perhaps they would benefit by having a more balanced spiritual development.

Ordinary Dreams

Almoli believes that there are different levels of dreaming and that not all dreams are alike. The type of dream one has is related to the type of conscious life that he or she has. Jung similarly recognized this relationship between the conscious and unconscious structures of the psyche and characterized it as compensatory: that is, dreams will often compensate for attitudes that may be missing from our waking consciousness.

For Almoli, a person's dreams reflect not only his spiritual level but also his attitude toward his dreams: "According to the degree of one's concern, so is his notification." The more we value the messages that our dreams bring, the more vital the communications that will be revealed to us.

Almoli reserves the prophetic dream for the true prophets and focuses his attention on the ordinary dream. Although he does not elevate the ordinary dream to the level of the prophetic dream, he does state that ordinary dreams are within the realm of prophecy, being "one-sixtieth part prophetic." One of the main distinctions between the two types of dreams is that prophetic dreams have powerful images that the dreamer clearly remembers, whereas ordinary dreams are often partially or totally forgotten. I have noticed that many patients bring into analysis fragments of dreams that they have mostly forgotten. By contrast, the ancient world, notably the Greeks, only interpreted "whole" dreams.

Almoli further points out that the prophetic dream contains no "useless material," whereas the ordinary dream comes with "a multitude of business." Although elsewhere in his book he contradicts this idea—remarking that what one interpreter finds useless, another interpreter may find useful—the observation seems valid. In the analysis of ordinary dreams, one often focuses on only a few of the dream images. Although the possibility exists of finding meaning in every dream image, the fact that many of these symbols remain uninterpreted makes them, from the viewpoint of consciousness, virtually useless.

Another important part of Almoli's definition of the ordinary dream is that it "does not originate in the will of the dreamer, for dreams do not come through one's choosing, but from the will of God." This is comparable to the Jungian notion that dreams are an example of the autonomous function of the unconscious. Dreams come from God and not from one's ego.

In postulating an active prophetic role for the ordinary dream, albeit on a individual level, Almoli was going against the talmudic notion that God's prophetic relationship with humanity ended after the destruction of the Holy Temple. Jewish philosophers such as Maimonides and Gersonides went to great theoretical lengths to banish ordinary dreams to a meaningless position in the governing of human thought and action. Maimonides denied that dreams could introduce new ideas or knowledge not previously known, declaring that they were simply the result of sense impressions gathered during waking hours and then acted upon by the imaginative faculty during sleep. Maimonides might be called a medieval forebear of the sleep-laboratory scientist trying to put his rational finger on the dream. Such an approach gives rise to a view of the dream that is divorced from the soul of the dreamer.

Although Maimonides was very careful to distinguish prophecy from ordinary dreams, he did allow the possibility that dreams could contain important matters to which God wanted to call the dreamer's attention. Two statements from *The Guide for the Perplexed* exemplify this position.

> . . . the phrase, "And Elohim (an angel) came to a certain person in the dream of night," does not indicate a prophecy, and the person mentioned in that phrase is not a prophet; the phrase only informs us that the attention of the person was called by God to a certain thing, and at the same time this happened at night. For just as God may cause a person to move in order to save or kill another person, so He may cause, according to His will, certain things to rise in man's mind in a dream by night.[14]

> . . . the prophecy revealed to Daniel and Solomon, although they saw an angel in the dream, was not considered by them a perfect prophecy, but as a dream containing correct information.[15]

In general, however, Almoli was up against a rationalistic philosophy that relegated the ordinary dream to matters of no consequence. If dreams were nothing but a rehashing of one's daily concerns, with no possibility of adding something new, why bother with them? Almoli probably had personal evidence that convinced him that experience disproves philosophical speculations on the nature of dreams. He was also fond of quoting literature that spoke of what individuals actually derive from their dreams, such as the cases of doctors who dreamed of hitherto unknown remedies and used them to heal their patients.

Almoli also seems to have been strongly influenced by what I term "the psychology of design." If God designed human beings to have ordinary dreams, then these dreams must have a purpose. Therefore, Almoli allows the possibility that ordinary dreams can contain new ideas, although he acknowledges that "these are few and far between."

Individual Destiny

The disregard of the revelatory potential of ordinary dreams on the part of philosophers like Maimonides points up another contrast between their way of thinking and Almoli's. The notion that God would concern Himself intimately with the everyday lives of ordinary individuals was foreign to most Jewish philosophers. Judaism has always emphasized the importance of the *people* of Israel—that is, of the collective rather than the individual. Almoli, however, was sensitive to the unique destiny of the individual. He believed that each individual has something special to contribute to humanity, and that the task of one's life is to discover what this contribution is and to actualize it. Almoli's philosophy is comparable to Jung's concept of individuation, the principle that the psyche strives for the completion and fulfillment of the individual personality. Both Almoli and Jung saw dreamwork as an aid to unfolding this important process.

For Jung, individuation was a psychological task of the second half of life, the first being taken up by the external goals of youth and young adulthood. Judaism, too, has its notion of specific tasks appropriate to specific stages of life. The Midrash refers to seven stages of life for a man:

> When he is one year old, he is compared to a king. He is placed in a canopied cradle and everyone embraces and kisses him.
>
> When he is two and three, he is likened to a pig. His hands are forever in foul places and everything he finds he places in his mouth.
>
> When he is ten, he jumps like a goat.
>
> When twenty, like a joyful, exuberant horse, he makes himself attractive and seeks a wife.
>
> When he marries he saddles himself and is like a donkey.
>
> When he has children, he has to humble himself like a dog to find sustenance for himself and his family.
>
> When he is old, he is like a monkey.[16]

Specific developmental stages for a scholar are given in the ethical treatise *Pirke Avot* ("Sayings of the Fathers"):

> At five years the age is reached for the study of Scripture; at ten for the study of the Mishnah; at thirteen for the fulfillment of the Commandments; at fifteen for the study of the Talmud; at eighteen for marriage; at twenty for understanding; at fifty for counsel; at sixty a man attains old age; at seventy the hoary head; at eighty the gift of special strength; at ninety he bends beneath the weight of his years; at a hundred he is as if he were already dead and had passed away from the world.[17]

Unfortunately, these texts do not give equal attention to the life stages of women. What is important, however, is the idea that, as a general rule, the lives of individuals move from one developmental stage to the next (an idea popularized in recent years by such books as Gail Sheehy's *Passages* and Daniel Levinson's *The Seasons of a Man's Life*), and the failure to adjust to a particular stage of life is often the cause of distress that sends people into psychotherapy. (I will discuss some dreams reflecting this problem in chapter 5.)

The notion of individuality has important implications for the art of dream interpretation. Almoli fully realized that each individual needs and is entitled to his or her own interpretation. The ability to see life as composed of individual natures is thus a cornerstone of the practice of counseling and dream interpretation.

Looking back on the beginnings of my own career in these fields, I realize that I was already very much concerned with the destiny of the individual while a young seminary student. For example, the highlight of my year was the High Holy Days, especially Yom Kippur, the Day of Atonement, because this seemed to be the only time of year when one could expect individual attention from God. Whereas holidays such a Chanukkah, Passover, and Purim celebrate God's intervention in the destiny of the Jewish people as a whole, the High Holy Days are a period of intense introspection concerning one's personal life. Yom Kippur is the last chance to repent of any wrongdoing before God determines one's destiny for the coming year, whether life or death, sickness or health, poverty or affluence. All of these human concerns are decided during a twenty-four-hour period, culminating with the Ne'ilah ("Closing") service, signifying that the gates of heaven are closed and the worshiper's fate has been sealed for the coming year. At the seminary I attended, Yom Kippur was the one day of the year when the emphasis was not on study but on piety. For me it was a remarkable experience. I would relish the hunger pangs of the fast and the physical stress of standing throughout the entire day of prayer. To this day I still have many dreams that take place on Yom Kippur. Traditionally, dreaming of Yom Kippur was considered inauspicious, but for me these dreams remind me positively of both my spiritual orientation as a Jew and my interest in individual destiny.

Besides Almoli, one can find here and there a traditional Jewish author who appreciates the inner call to individuation. One anecdote that I like comes from Reb Mendele of Kotzk, a nineteenth-century Chasidic rabbi. In a book called *The Culture of Compassion*, the role of individual destiny is explored in reference to some sayings of Reb Mendele. The tale is told:

> Once, when hearing an argument about which [of two men] was greater and how one can surpass another, the rebbe of Kotzk declared: "If I am I because I am I, and you are you because you are you, then I am I and you are you. But if I am I because you are you, and you are you because I am I, then I am not I and you are not you."[18]

In other words, if we sacrifice our inner direction for someone else's sake, then we cannot develop our own authentic selfhood.

When we speak of individual destiny, it is important to emphasize that this does not refer to a fixed, fated outcome. Jewish philosophy has always emphasized free will and the conviction that destiny is not carved in granite. The tablets of a foreboding destiny can be altered and even broken. Similarly, the promise or good potential of a situation may not be realized if we make no effort to achieve it. In a sense we struggle daily with our destiny, as we are continually being molded by predisposition or genetic factors combined with environmental and group or collective influences. The dream can be a vital force in the shaping of our destiny. I was once reminded of this idea by a dream in which I heard a voice saying, "It is possible to rewrite the script."

A legend about Moses seems to express this open-ended view of human potential:

> . . . [Moses] deserves more praise for his unusual strength of will than for his natural capacity, for he succeeded in transforming an originally evil disposition into a noble, exalted character, a change that was further aided by his resolution, as he himself acknowledged later. After the wonderful exodus of

> the Israelites from Egypt, a king of Arabia sent an artist to Moses, to paint his portrait, that he might always have the likeness of the divine man before him. The painter returned with his handiwork, and the king assembled his wise men, those in particular who were conversant with the science of physiognomy. He displayed the portrait before them, and invited their judgment upon it. The unanimous decision was that it represented a man covetous, haughty, sensual, in short, disfigured by all possible ugly traits. The king was indignant that they should pretend to be masters in physiognomy, seeing that they declared the picture of Moses, the holy, divine man, to be the picture of a villain. They defended themselves by accusing the painter in turn of not having produced a true portrait of Moses, else they would not have fallen into the erroneous judgment they had expressed. But the artist insisted that his work resembled the original closely.
>
> Unable to decide who was right, the Arabian king went to see Moses, and he could not but admit that the portrait painted for him was a masterpiece. Moses as he beheld him in the flesh was the Moses upon the canvas. There could be no doubt but that the highly extolled knowledge of his physiognomy experts was empty twaddle. He told Moses what had happened, and what he thought of it. He replied: "Thy artist and thy experts alike are masters, each in his line. If my fine qualities were a product of nature, I were no better than a log of wood, which remains forever as nature produced it as the first. Unashamed I make the confession to thee that by nature I possessed all the reprehensible traits thy wise men read in my picture and ascribed to me, perhaps to a greater degree than they think. But I mastered my evil impulses with my strong will, and the character I acquired through severe discipline has become the opposite of the disposition with which I was born. Through this change, wrought in me by my own efforts, I have earned honor and commendation upon earth as well as in heaven."[19]

In this legend we see the notion of the role of will combined with an individual's responsibility to transform his or her inherited nature and disposition through a conscious effort at development.

In Search of the Miraculous

The concept of destiny also relates to the idea of miracles in connection with Almoli's notion of God's role in the dreams of ordinary individuals. The belief in a God who is personally concerned with individual destiny creates the need to define what kinds of intercession humanity can expect from God.

The Talmud offers two guidelines for one's relationship to the miraculous. The first principle is that although it is permissible to pray for a miracle, one should not *rely* on the miraculous.[20] A Yiddish proverb states, "Dumplings in a dream are not dumplings, but a dream!"

The second principle relates to the private experiencing of a miraculous event.[21] Although in the history of the Jews there were many open, public miracles, such as the parting of the Red Sea, it later became accepted dogma that God no longer functions in this manner. The Talmud's assertion that miracles do not occur openly is related again to the basic notion of free will. The Bible reports God's words to His people: "I have set before you life and death, the blessing and the curse; therefore choose life" (Deut. 30:19). God wants us to choose life but does not force us to do so. Sensitive to the delicate relationship between faith and miracles, Jewish philosophers reasoned that if God were to appear openly to us, there would no longer be any possibility of choice, since we would feel obliged to conform to the divine directive. Out of compassion, God refrains from openly revealing Himself through miracles so that we can be rewarded for choosing the good.

If God's communication in dreams were obvious to everyone, we would forfeit the basic challenge of freely directing our own lives. Therefore, dreams allude to possibilities, but we have to decide how to utilize the allusions in the dream. As powerful tools of suggestion, dreams express potentialities but accomplish almost nothing without the dreamer's active response and participation. According to Almoli, the dream communication usually requires a prompt response, since the fulfillment of the dream is assumed to occur within the year. (The exception to this would be portents of one's status after death.)

In the *Sefer Chasidim* ("Book of the Pious"), it is written that if a man has an auspicious or positive dream, he should not tell it to his wife. The assumption was that she would tell her friends about it and thus God would cancel the boon promised by the dream, since He does not perform miracles openly. For Almoli, too, dreams had an element of privacy, as they represented a sacred communication between God and the individual. It is interesting to compare this approach with the contemporary example of analysts who ask their patients not to discuss their dreams outside of analysis.

Many people feel that if they dream about someone they know, they need to tell that person about the dream. Not only is this unnecessary, but it can even be harmful to the other person. I have seen numerous instances of people who used their dreaming of another person as a vehicle for their aggression. If I dream about you, it is my dream of you. Even if you are hurtful to me in the dream, it is still *my* dream. Although dreaming about your hurting me may reflect an objective situation or an appraisal from the unconscious of my relationship with you, that does not give me the automatic right to relate my dream to you. Dreams are to be treated like private letters that should be shared with discretion.

One night I had a dream of an analyst friend named John in which he expressed the optimistic idea to me that since I was a rabbi, I could do other things beside Jungian analysis. The next night, when my wife and I went to the movies, not only did we bump into John, but another couple we were with began talking about an old friend of theirs, who turned out to be John's father—two examples of the kind of meaningful coincidence that Jung termed "synchronicity." I thought of Almoli and the *Sefer Chasidim*, and I decided not to mention my dream to John. It was not important for John to know that I dreamed of him; it was important for me to understand the symbolic significance of dreaming of John's optimism.

I took the meaning of the dream and the synchronistic encounter as a reinforcement of my own resolve to work toward the synthesis of religion and healing. John was an ophthalmologist who had felt unfulfilled in his work and decided to study psychiatry and Freudian analysis. In my own life, I was working on reconnecting the fields of religion and healing. Since I was working on this book at the time, I felt that I should persevere in my efforts to understand those attitudes of the Jews toward dreams that might contribute insights to the dream analyst of today. I took the dream as unconscious support for my efforts in writing this book.

Which Dreams Should Be Interpreted?

There is one further category of ordinary dreams that deserves attention. Even though the Talmud states that "a dream which is not interpreted is like a letter which is not read," Almoli feels that not all dreams are meant for interpretation. The Talmud, too, seems to recognize this distinction when it states that the most significant dreams are those that occur close to waking.[22] It makes sense to me that the unconscious would select specific dreams for the dreamer's attention in this way. Sometimes patients bring to analysis a dream that occurred in the middle of the night and that was remembered simply because the dreamer happened to be awakened by a passing fire engine or some other disturbance. I usually feel that such dreams were not designed for analysis.

Although it has been clinically demonstrated that we need *all* of our dreams to maintain our sanity, the dreams of the middle of the night may be accomplishing their purpose without our conscious attention. Perhaps they have some automatic healing effect or serve a bookkeeping or filing-system function, enabling the mind to process an overload of information. I have often thought that dream laboratories in which subjects are awakened in the midst of dreaming are not studying dreams that are intended by the mind for interpretation. These researchers assume that dreams occurring under laboratory conditions are the same as those dreamed in a normal situation. It is my conviction that the unconscious is aware of the dreamer's situation and of the fate of the dream that it sends forth. The Master of Dreams is most certainly aware of who will be viewing or reviewing the dream.

It can be observed that the kinds of dreams that people have before entering analysis are different from the dreams that appear during the course of analysis. When a patient of mine dreams, I assume that his or her Master of Dreams knows that this dream will be brought to my attention. As the dream interpreter, I feel that the patient's unconscious dream-maker is addressing me as the one who will play an essential role in helping to make the dream a meaningful experience for the dreamer.

The Concerns of Dreams

When God communicates His will for an individual through dreams, what are the specific areas of life that He draws the dreamer's attention to? By reading through the dream-book section of Almoli's text, in which he offers meanings for particular symbols or images, I have culled a kind of "shopping list" of God's concerns for His creation. Here is a sampling of items from the list:

- life and death
- success and failure
- sickness and health
- poverty and affluence
- the status of one's *shalom bayit*: literally, the peace of one's house, or the question of whether one's house is in order
- whether to marry, stay married, or get divorced
- the choice of a husband or wife
- the marital relationship, including issues such as the health of one's spouse and adultery
- conception and pregnancy

- questions of timing, such as when to open a business, marry, have a child, etc.
- danger signals of impending disaster such as fire, impoverishment, or any reversal of fortune
- one's place in the world to come
- the fate of one's country
- the safety of one's environment or neighborhood
- the fate of one's enemies

The last three items on the list are notable in terms of Jewish history. For obvious reasons, Jews were concerned with their survival and safety in the various countries where they lived. Almoli himself was expelled from Spain around 1492. Jewish physical survival has often depended on the development of intuition, enabling people to know when it was time to leave an oppressive place for greener pastures.

Almoli seems to have been especially sensitive to dreams forecasting evil. There are numerous instances in which he advises the dreamer to recite a biblical verse that expresses the opposite of the bad forecast. This practice may serve to help the person keep an optimistic spirit while facing adversity. Maintaining a positive outlook is half the battle in dealing with any problem. It is the attitude expressed in the Talmud by the phrase *gam zu le-tovah*, "This also is for the good."[23]

One thing that is apparent from this list of concerns is that God is very much interested in our material well-being and the practical requirements of life. The divine plan for human beings includes not only faith in God and ethical, righteous conduct but also a life of prosperity in this world and the world to come. The consequence of not following the plan is a life of suffering, misery, and impoverishment in both worlds. The dream has the potential of helping individuals to manage their lives so as to ensure prosperity for all time.

Since many of the great *tzaddikim*, the saints of Judaism, endured much suffering and poverty, one might ask why their righteousness did not result in material well-being. The answer is that there are different forces at work in the lives of holy people as compared with ordinary folks. For the ordinary people with whom Almoli is concerned, there is ample evidence in the Jewish literature that suffering is undesirable and that poverty ought not to be romanticized or elevated to some divine status. The Jewish Bible finds it unthinkable to label a beggar a happy person, and the Talmud goes so far as to equate a poor man with a dead man. Just a few examples from the Book of Proverbs suffice to demonstrate the association of prosperity with goodness:

> I walk in the way of righteousness
> In the midst of the paths of justice,
> that I may cause those that love me to inherit substance
> and that I may fill their treasuries. (8:20–21)
> All the days of the poor are evil
> but he that is of a merry heart has a continual feast. (15:15)
> Love not sleep, lest you come to poverty;
> open thine eyes and you shall have bread in plenty. (20:13)
> He that follows after righteousness and mercy
> finds life, prosperity, and honor. (21:21)

In the Talmud, the same tractate that discusses dreams states: "Three things increase a man's self-esteem: a beautiful dwelling, a beautiful wife, and beautiful clothes."[24] The material and aesthetic dimension of life is linked with emotional well-being. My experience confirms that dreams often confront us with our material and aesthetic needs as well as with intellectual and spiritual insights.

The ancient Greeks also understood the relationship between wealth and well-being. They postulated that illness was equivalent to poverty and health to riches. Part of the cure that took place at the temples of Asclepius was a reversal of the fortunes of the dreamer from poverty to financial contentment. In his book on dream incubation in the ancient world, C. A. Meier writes:

> Poverty in the ancient world had all the dignity of a sickness . . . "illness and poverty" belonged together in religious

> thought just as did . . . "health and wealth," and were always cured at the same time. . . . If a person was cured of poverty in the Asclepieium, it generally happened by means of a dream *oracle* which led to the discovery of a hidden treasure.[25]

I am not saying that one must have a lot of money in order to be healthy, happy, or wise. However, there does seem to be a point along the economic continuum of our society at which a person is classified as "ill" in the financial realm. I am reminded of a Freudian analyst who sat next to me at a wedding once and told me that many of his patients came to him with lack of financial success as their chief complaint; he reported that he found these cases relatively easy to deal with. In my own practice, I have seen many people whose financial situation improved as a result of their work, in analysis, on dreams that point them in the direction of becoming successful in all areas of their lives. (See chapter 5 for some examples.)

The Moral Instinct in Dreams

In a famous story, a convert to Judaism challenged the great first-century sage Hillel to expound the whole of the Law while standing on one leg. Hillel's encapsulation of the Torah was: "What is hateful to you, do not do to your fellow man. That is the whole Law; the rest is interpretation."[26] Why didn't Hillel state this principle in the way that it is phrased in the Bible: "Love your neighbor as yourself" (Lev. 19:18)? A rational explanation of Hillel's phrasing is that individuals are more apt to be aware of what they don't want for themselves than of what they do want. I have often felt that the root of morality is the innate sense of fairness that we all have, an instinct for recognizing when we are being mistreated as well as when we are abusing others. As Jung wrote, "Man is a morally responsible being who, voluntarily or involuntarily, submits to the morality that he has created."[27] In the Jewish view, dreams play an important role in keeping us connected to this moral instinct.

A notable biblical example of a dream conveying the voice of conscience occurs during Abraham and Sarah's journey through the kingdom of Gerar. Since Sarah was so beautiful, Abraham knew that she was likely to be abducted, and if her abductors knew that Abraham was her husband, they would kill him. He therefore presented Sarah as his sister, so that at least his life would be spared. Sarah was then abducted for the harem of Abimelech, king of the Philistines. That same night, the king had a dream:

> But God came to Abimelech in a dream of the night and said to him: Behold, you will die, because of the woman whom you have taken; for she is a man's wife. Now Abimelech had not come near her; and he said: Lord, will you slay even a righteous nation? Did he not say to me: she is my sister? And she also said: he is my brother. It is with an innocent heart and pure hands that I did this. And God said to him in the dream: I knew that it was with an innocent heart that you did this, and I also withheld you from sinning against me. Therefore I did not allow you to touch her. Now go and return this man's wife, for he is a prophet, and he shall pray for you, and you shall live; and if you do not return her, know that you will surely die, you and all that are yours. (Gen. 20:3–7)

Some contemporary dream theorists deny that dreams have any moral content. Perhaps the question of the relationship between morality and dreaming depends on how we define morality. If we look at it in a broad sense, relating it to each person's unique situation, then dreams could be said to play a significant role in guiding individual moral development. There is a Jewish commentary on the Book of Job that speaks of the moral instinct reacting to the contents of dreams. The implication is that if a person is in contact with his moral instinct, he will know how to react to his dream. I have found numerous examples, in both my own and others' experience, of the voice of conscience in dreams and will recount some of them in chapter 5.

The Inner Child in Dreams

Another purpose of dreams is to keep us connected to our "inner child." It is common to dream of scenes of childhood and of oneself as a child. Such dreams may serve to reconnect us to the insights and emotional wisdom that we experienced when young. The psychoanalyst Ernst Kris's phrase "regression of ego in the service of ego" hints at the beneficial results of such a symbolic return to childhood.

The fact that children often possess wisdom beyond their years is widely recognized. A child's instinctual sense of fairness is a universal phenomenon, for example.[28] The need for a secure and stable home with two married parents will often lead children to sacrifice themselves for the preservation of family life, as has been well documented in the practice of family therapy. A famous literary demonstration of the true power of childhood understanding is *The Diary of Anne Frank*.

With their characteristic openness and spontaneity, children often remind us of truths that we may have forgotten as adults. The inner child within each adult can play the same role if we listen to its voice, which is often expressed in our dreams. The value of childhood insights for adults is suggested in the biblical verse "And he [Elijah] shall turn the heart of the fathers to the children, and the heart of the children to their fathers, lest I come and smite the land with utter destruction" (Mal. 3:24). Civilized man requires the synthesis of childhood and adult understanding in order to live constructively and avoid the pitfalls of human destructiveness.

The Symbolic Language of Dreams

The meaning of dream symbols is the subject of the second section of Almoli's book, which falls into the genre described by Jung as the "vulgar little dream book," with its ready-made generalizations. Actually, Almoli was well aware that the interpretation of a dream must take into account the dreamer's unique circumstances and cannot be based on an "A means B" type of equivalency. He expresses this notion in the following passage, which I have translated freely so as to bring out its strikingly modern perspective:

> It is impossible to enumerate the unlimited possibilities that can appear in dreams. One can only enumerate the primary areas and basic considerations. With this information the interpreter will be able to interpret any dream he encounters.
>
> It is well known that these generalized interpretations are not meant to be used with everyone. All interpretations must be weighed against the particular dreamer's general situation in life and his basic concerns, the context within which the dream occurred. These are determined by the interpreter's examination and evaluation.
>
> It is also important to realize that all of the dream interpretations we will discuss [i.e., in the dream-book section] are interpretations of ordinary matters that may appear in dreams. But interpreters must still discern and add from their own minds in order to understand the associations that come through the dream. One must go through this process in order to understand the dream in its entirety. This is because in any dream, one should first ascertain the parts of the dream and what each of them is pointing to. Those dream images that are not mentioned in this book must be understood through the Scriptures or one's own intuition. Once one understands what each part of the dream is pointing to, he still must imagine and reflect by means of his understanding and intelligence in order to reconcile the parts of the dream and thus to interpret it so that the entire dream will be pointing toward one matter and one happening. This can only be accomplished after the interpreter removes the useless material from the dream.

Although it is common today to discount dream-symbol dictionaries, they do have their own function and significance. Such books, which originate within a specific cultural milieu and are accepted by that group, represent a fascinating cultural achievement. Jung was sensitive to the fact that dream theory can vary from one culture to the next. He stated that his own dream theories were mainly heuristically valid and that he was ready to adapt them to the needs of any one patient, since each individual comes to dreamwork with his or her own family and cultural background. It is the hubris of modern dream research that it attempts to be purely scientific, as if the world were created in a laboratory without the rich variations that occur naturally in the human species. In fact, dream theories are never universally true but simply reflect the theoretician's personal, cultural, philosophical, and psychological bias. In this sense, Almoli's dream book should and does reflect a Jewish point of view, although not the only Jewish point of view.

The Talmud recognizes the principle that a knowledge of the dreamer's associations to the dream symbol is essential to understanding its meaning. For example, here is an excerpt on dreams of religious scholars, who would naturally be assumed to associate their dream images to familiar passages in the Bible:

> R. Joshua b. Levi said: If one sees a river in his dreams, he should rise early and say: *Behold I will extend peace to her like a river*, before another verse occurs to him, viz., *for distress will come like a river*. If one dreams of a bird he should rise early and say: *As birds hovering, so will the Lord of Hosts protect*, before another verse occurs to him, viz., *As a bird that wandereth from her nest, so is a man that wandereth from his place. . . .* If one dreams of a mountain, he should rise early and say: *How beautiful upon the mountains are the feet of the messenger of good tidings*, before another verse occurs to him, viz., *for the mountains will I take up a weeping and wailing. . . .*[29]

In this excerpt we also see a demonstration of the principle of interpreting dreams in a positive manner: the dreamer is reminded of a biblical verse that will ensure a beneficial association to the dream symbol.

Almoli cites an example from the Talmud that asserts that dreaming of a tree would mean one thing to a scholar and another to a thief.[30] For the scholar it is a symbol of being raised to a position of authority, while for the thief it is an omen of the gallows. Similarly, a dream about sexual intercourse would mean different things to different dreamers. If a man dreams of intercourse with a married woman, the Talmud states, he is assured of a place in paradise, but only if he does not know the woman about whom he dreamed and did not think of her the night before.[31] Almoli comments on this statement:

> It seems that this condition is applicable to all cases of having intercourse in dreams, for why should one instance be different from another? The explanation is based upon the principle that sexuality is one–sixtieth of the pleasures of paradise, and surely the more so with a married woman, where "stolen waters are sweeter" (Prov. 9:17). Furthermore, the dreamer is partaking of not only his own portion in paradise but also the portion of another, which is the case with a married woman [who also belongs to another].

The Talmud further says that if a man dreams of intercourse with his mother, "he may expect to obtain understanding, since it says, Yea, thou wilt call understanding 'mother' " (Prov. 2:3 with a slight change of reading). And if he dreams of intercourse with his sister, "he may expect to obtain wisdom, since it says, Say to wisdom, thou art my sister" (Prov. 7:4).[32]

To convey the flavor of Almoli's dictionary of dream symbols, here is my translation of his section on dreams about the dead.

> If one sees his dead relative coming to visit him, wealth will come to him. And the more so if the relative embraces and kisses him. But if the deceased bites him, a calamity will pass over him.
>
> If a dead person gives him anything, a gain will come to him. But if the gift is something whose first letter is *nun* or *lamed*, he will succumb to poverty. [The Hebrew word for "poverty" has the letter *nun* within it, and the word for "succumb" begins with a *lamed*.]
>
> If the dead are stealing from the living, one of his relatives will die. But if the dead are giving to the living implements of

iron or weapons of war, wherever he travels, he can rest assured and there is no apprehension (Rabbenu Chai).

But Rashi states: If the dead gives him anything and he refuses to receive it, something bad will happen.

If the dreamer sees his father or mother dead, if the dream occurs after their actual death, rejoicing will come to him. And if they give him something, the rejoicing will be greater.

If he sees himself washing, dressing, or carrying the dead, he will lose status.

If he is visiting people after they have died or consoling mourners, an event will transpire in which God will come close to him (Rabbenu Chai).

If he sees a person murdered, a miracle will occur.

If he sees graves, ugly events will come to pass.

The Talmud says: If he sees a eulogy, heavenly protection will be bestowed upon him, but only if the eulogy is in written form.

If the dreamer is speaking with the Angel of Death, he will get sick but recuperate.

But if the angel is standing near his head, he will die.

If the angel is standing by his feet, he will fall ill and approach death, and then will be healed.

If he sees himself dead, an event will occur to bring him close to God, blessed be He. This is also the case if he sees the shrouds of the dead.

If he sees himself in a coffin and in the ground, some anguish will pass over him, and perhaps he may be saved.

Rabbenu Chai: If he sees himself in a grave, he will be handed over to someone cruel.

If he is living in a cemetery, he will soon be living in prison.

Daniel says: If one sees himself dead, his life will be lengthened.

The Talmud says: "Our Rabbis taught: [If one dreams of] a corpse in the house, it is a sign of peace in the house; if that [the corpse] was eating and drinking in the house, it is a good sign for the house; if that he took articles from the house, it is a bad sign for the house. Rabbi Papa explained it to refer to a shoe or sandal. Anything that the dead person [is seen in the dream] to take away is a good sign except a shoe and a sandal;

> anything that it puts down is a good sign except dust and mustard" (*Berakhot* 57b). The explanation is that when his shoes and sandals are removed, it is a sign that the master of the household is going together with him either by foot or by the loss of one's foothold on the streets. The dust is the sign of burial. Mustard [powder] is also symbolic of this, as it is fine like dust.
>
> If the dreamer sees dead people in dreams, he need not be apprehensive if he is healthy; but if he is sick, it will be bad for him.
>
> If he is conversing with a dead person, he should associate himself with good people and emulate them.

In order to understand the rationale behind such interpretations, it is necessary to know something about Jewish attitudes toward death and mourning. To shed some light on the symbolic representations of Jewish culture, let's examine one item from Almoli's list: the paragraph from the Talmud about dreaming of a corpse in the house.

The Jewish custom is to divide mourning into three periods. During the initial, seven-day period ("sitting *shivah*"), which is the most intense, the mourners stay at home and abstain from working, remove their shoes, and sit on low stools. This is followed by a less severe period covering the next twenty-three days. The remainder of the first year after the death constitutes the third and lightest mourning period.

The practice of sitting *shivah* is psychologically very sound, as it requires the family to cease all worldly activity so that they can properly grieve over their loss. The custom of removing the shoes is possibly a symbolic gesture of support for or unity with the deceased, who is also struggling to separate from the living and to set out on his or her eternal road. After seven days, however, the survivors must put their shoes back on and reenter the world of the living. The Talmud seems to be saying that dreaming of a dead person in your house is a good sign because it means that you are not repressing the memory of your loved one. Your house is said to be at peace. The word for peace, *shalom*, also denotes wholeness or completeness, so there is also the suggestion of psychological health.

It is also possible that our preoccupation with the deceased may pull us out of worldly life, so that we take the mourning process to an unhealthy extreme. A person in a state of pathological mourning may find himself unable to stop thinking about the deceased, may withdraw from customary activities, including eating, and may even die. It is not uncommon to hear about the sudden demise of an elderly person whose long-time spouse had recently died. If the dead appear in a dream and rob you of your shoes or leave the dust of the earth on your doorstep, this could symbolize that you are in an abnormally prolonged state of mourning or that your relationship to your deceased relatives or ancestors has become morbid. (Of course, this interpretation would be valid only if this particular mourning custom were part of your cultural background or way of life.)

Notice in the above passage that word play—in this case involving the Hebrew word *shalom*—can be an important part of dream symbolism. The Talmud contains numerous examples. It tells of one dream in which the dreamer's nose fell off; this was interpreted to mean, "Fierce anger has been removed from you," because the Hebrew word for "nose" (*af*) also means "anger."[33] Almoli cites a dream from the Midrash that involves punning in Greek (see page 16).

Freud wrote of similar insights into dream puns in his own practice of dream interpretation. One of his patients dreamed of going to Italy—*gen Italien* in German; Freud interpreted this as an allusion to the sexual organs—*Genitalien*.[34]

One of my own dream provides an interesting example of Hebrew word play. In the dream, I am in a hospital room in a Nazi prison building with many floors. I seem to be observing a couple: the woman gets bored with staying in the room and leaves to go for a walk. After she returns, the prison guard, who has observed her action, comes to take her away. When he arrives, the man points to a young man in the room and says, "We have called you Penuel and empowered you for times like this."

The young man understands that his task now is to murder the guard. I wonder how they will conceal the dead body.

After recording this dream, I wondered about the meaning of "Penuel." The word literally connotes turning to God (*panu*, turn; *el*, God). I reflected that turning to God is what is needed when dealing with one's shadow, or the dark side of the personality ("Nazis"). I also considered that the dream might be showing me the idea of divine concern, which is the underlying purpose of dreaming. Since I was working on this book at the time, the dream seemed to indicate that my unconscious was participating in the endeavor.

I also associated the dream to a passage in the Bible about the place where Jacob wrestled with the angel: "And Jacob called the name of the place Peniel ["the face of God"]: 'for I have seen God face to face, and my life is preserved' " (Gen. 32:31). Although in my dream the name is Penuel, not Peniel, my association to this passage also supports the insight that dreams can promote a positive attitude of dependence on divine guidance.

"The dream is the unripe fruit of prophecy," states the Midrash Rabbah. I find this image of the dream as an "unripe" or unfinished product very provocative, inviting the question, "How do I ripen or complete the dream?" It is interpretation that makes the dream ripe, or at least gives it the possibility of ripening. If the dream is the unripe fruit, then interpretation is the harvesting and marketing. The essential role of the interpreter in this process, which leads to the dream's fulfillment, is the subject of the next chapter.

4. The Dream Interpreter

A frequently quoted passage from the Talmud states that "a dream that is not interpreted is like a letter that is not read." For Almoli, the failure to interpret a dream was a guarantee of not deriving any benefit from the dream, for, he says, "dream communications are given to man with the understanding that they will be interpreted." Jewish dream theory is founded on the basic requirement of interpreting the dream rather than simply taking it as an objective statement on its own.

Closely related to this principle is the idea that the dreamer cannot adequately interpret his or her own dream. Almoli implies that interpretation can only be entrusted to someone who is not only learned and wise but also objective. This insight is indicated in the Talmud as well, where the analogy is used that it is difficult to be simultaneously on the ground and on the roof.[1] In order to understand a dream, the interpreter must be at a distance. Recall that a dream is not merely a self-picturing device focused on the present; it also has an eye for the future possibilities of the dreamer—what Jung called the prospective function. The conscious mind has a natural resistance to "rocking the boat" with change, even if it is a needed change. The dream interpreter can make a more objective evaluation of what the dream is saying, as he or she does not share the dreamer's resistance.

The Talmud states: "If one has a dream which makes him sad, he should go and have it interpreted. . . ."[2] Note that the kind of dream that is to be brought for interpretation is one that evokes anxiety. The Bible has numerous examples of dreamers—such as Pharaoh and Nebuchadnezzar—who are upset by their dreams and frantically search for an explanation that will relieve their anguish. The role of interpreter, then, is to help alleviate distress. Just as in ancient times, people today tend to bring their "bad" dreams to the analyst. Rarely do any of my patients tell me about a "good" dream. After all, they are consulting a therapist in the first place because something is troubling them.

The ancients in general assumed that the dream had a problem-solving function. In classical Greece, dreams were the focus of a healing ritual that took place at the sanctuaries devoted to the god Asclepius. These were sacred places where people could incubate or induce a healing dream. After performing the appropriate rituals, they would go to sleep in the sanctuary. The god would appear in some form in a dream and tell the dreamer what remedy was needed; in some cases the epiphany of the god was itself the healing event. Here the role of the dream interpreter (when there was one) was simply to listen to the dream and acknowledge the healing elements or the cure that was sure to follow. The interpreter was thus a mediator between the dreamer and the god who sent the dream.

The Jewish dream interpreter performed a similar role, as suggested by Almoli's original title for his book, "Dream Mediator." The Jews were always concerned with the purpose of phenomena and with the intentions that God has for His creatures. It was therefore natural for the Jews to assign a meaningful purpose to dreams. The Jewish dream interpreter was like a sacred technician who probed the dream in order to extract from it the particular will or destiny that God wanted for the dreamer. The interpreter would not simply acknowledge the message of the dream but would actively formulate and recommend a solution to the dreamer's problem as expressed in the dream.

Who Interprets?

Among the ancients the task of interpretation rested unequivocally with the interpreter. However, he could not exercise his problem-solving skills without the assistance of the dreamer. Almoli emphasizes that it is not enough to know the meaning of symbols in the abstract; one must be informed of the dreamer's life situation. We might even say that the interpreter does not just interpret a dream; he interprets the *life* of the dreamer through the dream. Dream interpretation is really a collaborative endeavor, relying on the cooperation of the dreamer, who must supply the necessary information so that the interpreter can make effective use of his skills. As in other forms of healing work, the interpreter needs continuous feedback from the dreamer to guide the work of healing.

Freud placed most of the responsibility for interpretation on the dreamer, at least early in the development of his dream theory. "The technique which I describe . . . differs in one essential aspect from the ancient method," he wrote; "it imposes the task of interpretation on the dreamer himself. It is not concerned with what occurs to the interpreter in connection with a particular element of the dream, but with what occurs to the dreamer."[3] Jung acknowledged that "it is Freud's great achievement to have put dream interpretation on the right track. Above all, he recognized that no interpretation can be taken without the dreamer."[4] Eventually, however, both men modified their views. Freud later wrote, "We are thus obliged . . . to adopt a combined technique, which on one hand rests on the dreamer's associations and on the other hand fills the gaps from the interpreter's knowledge of symbols."[5] Jung, too, with his technique of amplification, allowed for the analyst to contribute his own experience and understanding of myth and symbol.

Theory does not always correspond to practice, and in actuality we often find that the interpreter does most of the interpreting. The Jungian analyst Robert A. Johnson has described a revealing encounter with Jung:

> Dr. Jung took me into the garden and proceeded to give me a very long lecture on the meaning of my dream, what it meant to me to have contact in this manner with the deep parts of the collective unconscious, how I should live, what I might expect of my life, what I should not attempt, what I could trust, what did belong to me in life. The meeting took nearly three hours

> and it was clear that I was to listen and not interrupt. Nondirective counselling, indeed! Dr. Jung advised me to spend most of my time alone, have a separate room in the house to be used for nothing but inner work, never to join any organization or collectivity. He indicated that though it was true I was a young man, my dream was of the second half of life and was to be lived no matter what age I was. When such a dream comes it is to be honored whether the time or the circumstances are convenient or not. Dr. Jung told me that the unconscious would protect me, give me everything I needed for my life, and that my one duty was to do my inner work. All else would follow from this. He said that it was not the least important whether I accomplished anything outwardly in this life since my one task was to contribute to the evolution of the collective unconscious. . . .[6]

I heard a similar story from a trainee at the C.G. Jung Institute in Zurich, who told me about his first session with one of the prestigious analysts there. After he had presented his dream, the analyst asked him a few personal questions. She then spent the next hour telling him what she understood about him based on the dream. She took care to warn him first that, since she had only just met him, her interpretation might be off; nevertheless, she did not hesitate to advise him on what course of action to take for his future benefit.

Obviously the Jungians have not deviated very far from the ancient conception of dream mediator. For the modern-day analyst the dream carries the voice of the soul, urging us on to psychological maturity, spiritual growth, and the discovery of meaning.

A Joint Effort

Almoli is sensitive to the cooperative nature of dream work. He sees dream interpretation as a joint effort of three parties: the dreamer, the divine voice of the dream, and the dream interpreter, who elicits the divine guidance from the dream. Almoli is also aware of the ways in which dreams are affected by variables such as the dreamer's attitude toward his dreams, the skills of the dream interpreter, and God's attitude toward the dreamer.

According to Almoli, one must first consider the basic attitude of the dreamer toward his dreams, which can be classified as either cooperative or uncooperative. People who think that dreams are useless meanderings of the mind are unlikely to profit from having their dreams interpreted. However, those who feel that the potential for divine guidance can be found within dreams are in a good position to benefit from the services of a dream interpreter.

The manner in which people treat their own dream material reflects their attitudes toward dreams. Almoli cites biblical sources concerning the handling and transcribing of dreams, as found in the stories of Joseph, Jacob, and Nebuchadnezzar, and then concludes that "one should safeguard and remember one's dreams in meticulous detail." People who keep a careful record of their dreams will get more out of consulting an interpreter, since they have the raw material that he needs in order to advise them. Almoli goes on to state this equation: "According to one's degree of concern, so is his notification." If God sees that the dreamer is unconcerned and attributes no value to his dreams, He will cease to communicate anything essential and will transmit only insignificant things. Stated in secular terms, if we pay attention to our dreams and honor their point of view, we will receive more helpful communications from the unconscious through dreams.

The cooperation of God is very important. The Talmud states, "If one goes seven days without a dream, he is called evil."[7] According to one commentary, the absence of dreaming reflects God's lack of concern for the well-being of the dreamer. Today it is recognized that the experience of having no dreams is more likely to be a failure to *remember* the dreams that one did have. In modern terms we might say that a person who goes a long time without a dream may be someone who is not remembering and listening to his dreams, and who is therefore out of touch with his unconscious. Such a person would be missing the positive feedback that comes through the creative union of the conscious and unconscious worlds.

Almoli elaborates on his theory that the ability to derive value from dreams depends directly on the dreamer's cooperative attitude toward the dream communication: "Once a dreamer becomes involved with his dreams and seeks to interpret them clearly, he should work at fulfilling their messages. Since this work is necessary in dealing with all dreams, and since without this work a dream is virtually meaningless, Joseph was compelled to advise Pharaoh of the means for fulfilling his dream." For Almoli, the dream requires the dreamer to act on its message, following the advice of the interpreter.

The Dream Interpreter as Advisor

In Almoli's theory, the roles of dream interpreter and advisor are closely linked. Actually, it is the dream itself which is the advisor; the interpreter simply seeks to give voice to it. To put this another way, the dream is the source of information or wisdom upon which the interpreter bases his advice.

The Bible is full of stories related to the notion of the good versus the bad advisor. Pharaoh's wise men and Nebuchadnezzar's counselors were shown to be poor advisors, whereas Joseph and Daniel were good advisors. What are the qualifications—the special skills, talents, and personality traits—that make a good advisor?

Joseph is the earliest biblical example of a dream interpreter and a model of the profession. We are fortunate in having a fairly elaborate portrayal of Joseph's early life in the Book of Genesis. Joseph began life with some real problems. He was the older son of his mother, Rachel (whose other son was Benjamin). Rachel was favored by her husband, Jacob, over his other wife, Leah, who had six sons. (Jacob also had four sons by two of his concubines.)

> Now Israel [Jacob] loved Joseph more than any of his children since he was the child of his old age. He made him a colorful coat. When his brothers saw that his father loved him more than all his brothers, they hated him and could not speak peaceably to him. Now Joseph had a dream, and when he told it to his brothers they only hated him the more. (Gen. 37:3–4)

Being the favorite child inflated Joseph's ego and made him the object of rage and envy. In this difficult situation he turned to his inner life, the world of his dreams; but this got him into more trouble, since the dreams he reported reflected his inflated sense of destiny. In one dream, he saw sheaves in a field bowing down to his own sheaf; in another, he saw the sun, moon, and eleven stars bowing down to him. Joseph's eleven brothers recognized the meaning of these dreams and taunted him, "Do you want to be our king?" Jacob, too, scolded Joseph but suspended judgment. Today, Joseph would probably be diagnosed as suffering from a narcissistic personality disorder. From the religious point of view, Joseph—who is known as ha-Tzaddik, the Righteous—did have an exalted destiny in relation to the fate of the Jewish people. In any case, the task for Joseph was to turn his difficult set of circumstances into something positive.

But first, things got worse. Joseph's brothers plotted to murder him. They threw him into a dry well and left him to die, but later decided to sell him to the Arabs instead. Thus Joseph became a slave of Potiphar, one of Pharaoh's officers in Egypt. Once more Joseph found himself favored, and he was appointed his master's personal servant. But when Potiphar's wife tried to seduce Joseph and failed, she had him thrown into prison. Again Joseph turned to his inner life and intuitions. Because of his correct interpretations of the dreams of his fellow prisoners, he was freed. Now that Joseph had made a name for himself as a dream interpreter, when Pharaoh had a disturbing dream and could find no one to explain it satisfactorily, he summoned Joseph. As a result of his interpretation, Joseph was put in charge of the entire land of Egypt, was able to ease the famine predicted in Pharaoh's dream, and was reunited with his family.

The story of Joseph suggests that a good advisor is one who has learned to transform personal problems into the shaping of his or her destiny. Joseph learned the art of following his destiny through this kind of creative problem solving and eventually combined his talent in understanding dreams with the role of advisor to the king. A similar gift for resourcefulness in the face of difficulty is exemplified by a healer of our own time, Milton Erickson, the founder of modern clinical hypnosis. Although disabled from polio, Erickson undertook a difficult canoe trip and thereby learned the art of problem solving and survival.[8] Perhaps this heroic journey predestined him to devote his life to helping others to solve their problems. Erickson went on to develop the field of hypnotherapy and also influenced the work of Jay Haley, who developed a system of strategic psychotherapy for families in crisis. Success in mastering one's own life difficulties leads to confidence in one's ability to help others in distress.

The Luck Factor

Joseph's ability to be successful at whatever he undertook represents another aspect of the dream interpreter's profile. We read that "the Lord was with Joseph, and he became a successful man; and he was in the house of his master the Egyptian, and his master saw that the Lord was with him, and the Lord caused all that he did to prosper in his hands" (Gen. 39:2–4). This lucky "Midas touch" of Joseph's was the reason why he was sought after as a dream interpreter. The dream interpreter who is a failure in personal and business life is not likely to instill the confidence in his abilities that will attract clients.

Many Jungian analysts believe that one cannot help another person beyond one's own level of psychological development. In essence, he who cannot help himself in some area of his own life should not set himself up to help others in that area. This principle is talmudic: Justify your own life before you attempt to justify the lives of others.[9] It thus follows that the dream interpreter who is an expert in the "luck factor" will be able to lead his clients to become lucky or successful in their own lives. Almoli believed that dream interpretation could help dreamers to reverse the course of their lives from evil to good, from catastrophe to success, from poverty to affluence, from sickness to health. Implicit in the Jewish view of dreams as communications from God is the optimistic notion that individuals have the ability to solve and transform their life dilemmas.

The Wounded Healer

Looking at the other side of the coin, one is often struck by the problematic personal lives of psychotherapists and other counselors. Jokes are often told about the children of "shrinks," as if everyone expects the offspring of therapists to exhibit severe disorders. The truth is that so-called normal people do not gravitate to the field of psychotherapy. The saying "It takes one to know one" is the key to understanding this phenomenon—and perhaps points to one of the personality traits of the successful dream interpreter.

In Jungian psychology, the archetypal image of the "wounded healer"—expressed in the myth of the centaur Chiron, for example—reflects this notion that a healer is often one who has confronted and worked through his or her own suffering. In recognition of this fact, Freud required that people who want to become psychoanalysts should first, as part of their training, undergo their own personal analysis. The training analysis can help in three ways. One, the trainees will learn what it means and feels like to undergo psychoanalysis. Two, they can observe the manners and style of a seasoned analyst and experience the therapeutic value of self-reflection in the presence of a professional who practices the art of healing by listening, talking, and interpreting. Three, the analysis helps the trainees to work through some of their own neurotic entanglements that would hinder their capacity to function as healers. In order to withstand the daily barrage of influences coming from their patients' neurotic or pathological states, psychotherapists need to be grounded in their own being, with a clear awareness of their own weaknesses and strengths. The greater a therapist's self-awareness, the more likely it is that he or she will operate in a healing rather than a destructive manner.

There is an interesting Chasidic tale entitled "His Only Failing":

> An ailing man came to the Yud [a Chasidic rabbi] and asked him to pray for his health. The Yud told him to make the request of a man by the name of Shalom, in an adjacent town. There the only Shalom was a drunkard who lived on the outskirts of the town in a miserable hut. The man waited until he became sober, and then made his request. The drunkard asked for a gallon of brandy, and after receiving it, advised the man to bathe in a river, and he would be cured. This proved to be correct.
>
> When meeting the Yud later, the man asked the Rabbi why he had sent him to a drunkard. The Rabbi replied:
>
> "Shalom, my friend, has an exceedingly kind nature, and he oftentimes helps people when he is able to do so. His only fault is a love of strong drink, but this craving saves him from every other sin."[10]

Although alcoholism is no doubt as undesirable in a therapist as in anyone else, this story does show that healers do not need to be perfect in order to heal successfully. What they do need is a high degree of self-awareness and sensitivity to individual destiny.

Healers have their own need to concern themselves with distressed individuals. Psychotherapists are attracted to psychopathology and to people with problems, which constitutes their life's work. For me, as a psychotherapist, "normal" people (if there are any) have no real fascination. I find them unexciting, predictable, and often boring. But give me a neurotic, and I am like a cat who sees a mouse: my analytic mind lights up with everything it has to offer, my problem-solving fantasies are constellated, and I feel energized and ready to go to work. Psychotherapists, like other providers of services, are attracted to those who need the service they are offering. A psychotherapist should never underestimate the fact that his patients provide him with his livelihood.

Qualifications of the Healer

Another implication of the Chasidic tale quoted above is the need for clients to concern themselves with the effectiveness of psychotherapy rather than with the superficial elements in the therapist-patient relationship. The primary issue in psychotherapy is whether the patient receives benefit from the treatment. When I function as a psychotherapist, I am focused more on what is going on in the patient's life than on my technique. The most therapeutic aspect of the psychotherapist's personality is this ability to focus upon the life of another, which in turn facilitates the patient's own self-awareness.

One of the saddest individuals that I have treated, the daughter of a psychotic mother and a depressed father, found it intolerable to have my attention directed toward her. She experienced it as a rape of her personality. Her feelings of inferiority were so powerful that she imagined that any attention she received was negative. It took many years for her to be able to accept personal attention as a nourishing experience.

The healing effect of one soul upon another is a direct result of the focusing, concern, awareness, and understanding that a psychotherapist communicates to his or her patient. Often, this communication is subliminally transferred from the unconscious of the healer to the unconscious of the patient, and this exchange constellates or arouses the patient's inner healer. The ability to stimulate the inner healer of the patient is an indispensable qualification of any healer, including the dream interpreter.

One of the goals of psychotherapy is to help people to meet their needs. Often, however, patients are unaware of their needs;

they got to a therapist because of a feeling of general frustration and unhappiness, and have not defined their problem beyond that. The role of the dream interpreter or therapist, then, may be to help them to identify unfulfilled needs that they are currently unaware of. This notion was expressed by a Chasidic *rebbe*, Moshe Leib of Sasov:

> How to love a man is something I learned from a peasant. I was at an inn where peasants were drinking. For a long time all were silent until one person, moved by the wine, asked a man sitting beside him, "Tell me, do you love me or don't you?" The other replied, "I love you very much." The intoxicated peasant spoke again, "You say that you love me but you do not know what I need; if you really loved me, you would know." The other had not had a word to say to this and the peasant who put the question fell silent again. But I understand the peasant; for to know the needs of men and to help them bear the burden of their sorrow, that is the true love of man.[11]

The practice of dream interpretation requires a knowledge of such human needs. The dreams themselves are what help the interpreter to understand the dreamer's needs. There is a story of a patient who consulted with Jung about some personal problem and then asked Jung, "Doctor, do you think you can help me?" Jung responded, "I don't know yet. I first have to see what your dreams are saying."

Until a dreamer realizes that he is unable to interpret his own dreams, he will usually miss the meaning of his dream communication. Many individuals suffer from what might be termed "the Jonah syndrome": they continually engage in escapist activities. This behavior is often reflected in their dreams, but it usually requires a dream interpreter to bring this message home to their consciousness. Part of the interpreter's art is the ability to convince the dreamer of what the dream is trying to communicate. Since dreams are often the voice of the higher self in the role of critical observer of the actions, emotions, and thoughts of the dreamer's conscious life, the interpreter must function as a benevolent critic.

Almoli rightly felt that the essential role of the dream interpreter is not to be a prophet of doom but to advise people so that they can achieve the good things that life has to offer. Advisors are problem solvers, not problem creators, and psychotherapists should not create difficulties by bringing more problems to the patient's conscious awareness than he or she is capable of resolving.

Although at times dreams seem to be conveying a painful message to the dreamer I work under the assumption that if the unconscious presents a dream, the dreamer is ready to explore the contents of that dream and to hear its interpretation. The exceptions to this principle are the initial dream that a patient presents and any dreams from before the analysis. Again I want to stress that the unconscious is fully aware of the specific dream interpreter who will be helping the dreamer to make the dream a meaningful experience. The interpreter's responsibility is to offer the interpretation in a helpful style, to ensure that the dream becomes a positive force in the dreamer's life.

Learning how to offer interpretations and how to advise people is an essential element in dream interpretation. Professional dream interpreters should be comfortable with people and their problems and with the process of change and transformation. They should have respect for the unique individuality of people and their destinies. But more than anything, the skillful dream interpreter is an experienced problem solver who approaches human dilemmas with a basic optimism. He or she realizes that identifying a problem prematurely can ensure that the problem will never be solved.

When I first started doing psychotherapy as a chaplain in the army, I saw a woman whose presenting problem was that she was repeatedly sexually abused by the postman after he rang her doorbell and she let him in. My first response was to ask her why she didn't put a chain on her door and monitor the caller before letting him in. This advice was premature, as the woman was already aware of this obvious solution but was unable to apply it because of her masochistic behavioral patterns.

She rightfully realized that I did not understand her problem, and my simplistic advice resulted in the termination of the psychotherapy. Before attempting to solve the problem, I should have first given her a sense that I comprehended the situation and her inability to solve the problem on her own. Later she might have been more open to any solutions that I might suggest.

Vocational Hazards

Modern dream theories are usually an attempt to find "the" interpretation. Freud, for example, wrote:

> . . . you will point to having heard that one is seldom certain that the interpretation arrived at is the only possible one, and there is danger of overlooking another perfectly admissible interpretation of the same dream. . . . If for the "arbitrary decision" of the interpreter you will substitute his skill, his experience and his understanding, then I am with you. This kind of personal factor is indispensable, especially when interpretation is difficult; it is just the same in other scientific work, however; it can't be helped that one man will use any given technique less well, or apply it better, than another. *The impression of arbitrariness* made, for example, by the interpretation of symbols is corrected by the reflection that as a rule the connection of the dream-thoughts with one another, and of the dream with the life of the dreamer and the whole mental situation at the time of the dream, points directly to *one* of all possible interpretations and renders all the rest useless.[12]

Jung was also sensitive to this dilemma. He attempted to find meaning in the whole dream, as if the dream were one single story. Jung had a test for determining the accuracy of his interpretation; if the interpretation was wrong, it would not "click" with the analysand. As a further check, Jung felt that if his interpretation was wrong, subsequent dreams of the same dreamer would show him that he was in error. He also realized that one reaches different interpretations depending on one's point of view.

Jung's concern over the issue of wrong interpretations points to a basic vocational hazard. There is no surefire way of getting around the problem, except to face the fact that dream interpretation is a fallible profession. The interpreter does his best but is far from perfect. Recognizing the fallibility of the dream interpreter helps us to put the art in a more realistic light. One of the dangers of this work is that the interpreter may acquire an inflated view of himself as the expert who knows all. Almoli's position was that the interpreter must realize that every dream has numerous indications, and the fact that he notices one of them does not mean that no other interpretations exist. Acknowledging that his insights into the dream are based on his own subjective viewpoint, he should voice his interpretations in terms of possibilities rather than facts.

There is a fascinating Jewish legend about some of the dangers of being a healer, which can also be applied to the dream interpreter's situation. In this tale we are also introduced to the complex relationships that exist between a healer and his own dreams and between the verbal and nonverbal elements in the healing. In addition, the tale expresses the notion of allowing the healer to do his work without complaining about the details of the treatment.

According to the legend, when the king of Persia was deathly ill, his physicians prescribed the milk of a lioness to heal him. The king therefore sent his servants to Solomon to find out how they could get this remedy. Solomon summoned a Jewish physician, with whose help they obtained the milk. While they were on their way back to the king, the physician had a dream that the parts of his body were arguing with one another:

> The feet were saying: "Among all the parts, there are none like us. Had we not walked, he would not have been able to fetch any of the milk."
>
> The hands replied, saying: "There are none like us. Had we

not touched the lioness, he would not now be carrying any of the milk."

The eyes said: "We are of greater worth than any of you. Had we not shown him the way, nothing at all would have been accomplished."

The heart spoke, saying: "I am of greater worth than any of you. Had I not given counsel, you would not have succeeded at all in the errand."

But the tongue spoke up and said: "I am better than you. Had it not been for speech what would you have done?"

Then all the parts replied, saying to the tongue: "Art thou not afraid to compare thyself with us, thou that art lodged in a place of obscurity and darkness—thou indeed in whom there is not a single bone such as there is in all the other parts?"

But the tongue declared: "This very day, you are going to acknowledge that I rule you."

As the physician woke up from sleep, he kept the dream in his heart, and went on his way. He came to the king, and said: "Here is the milk of a bitch which we went to get for thee. Drink it."

Immediately the king became angry with the physician and ordered that he be hanged. As he went out to be hanged, all the parts began to tremble. The tongue said to them: "Did I not tell you this day, that there is nothing to you? If I save you now, will you admit that I rule you?"

They said: "Yes."

Then the tongue said to those who were about to hang the physician: "Bring me back to the king." They brought the physician back to the king, and he asked the king: "Why didst thou order to have me hanged?"

The king replied: "Because thou broughtest the milk of a bitch to me."

He asked the king: "What does that matter to thee? It will cure thee. Besides, a lioness can be called a bitch."

The king then took some of the milk, and drank, and was healed. And so, since it was proved that the milk was the milk of a lioness, the physician was dismissed in peace.

Thereupon all the parts said to the tongue: "Now do we

> confess to thee that thou rulest all the parts." Of this it is written *Death and life are in the power of the tongue* (Prov. 18:21). And so David declared: I said: "*I will take heed to my ways, that I sin not with my tongue.*"[13]

If this physician had heeded the message of his dream, he would have realized that he was dangerously inflated with the belief that the king's healing was due to his own merit. By contrast, the biblical dream interpreters Joseph and Daniel acknowledged that their problem-solving powers came from God. In Daniel there was said to be "the spirit of the holy gods" (Dan. 5:11), and before offering his account and interpretation of Nebuchadnezzar's dream, Daniel praised God as the source of all wisdom and understanding (Dan. 2:19ff). Joseph also considered himself a channel of divine wisdom, telling Pharaoh's officers who came to him with their dreams, "Do not interpretations belong to God?" (Gen. 40:8). The skillful dream interpreter never takes credit for his success but attributes his intuitive powers to the divine forces operating within him.

Another occupational hazard arises from the dream interpreter's continuous proximity to the dream world. He spends much of his time deciphering the meaning of people's dreams and moving in and out of their souls. This intimate contact with the inner lives of others makes it imperative that the dream interpreter be grounded in the meaning of his own existence. Otherwise, he runs the risk of being carried away into the soul (or even the body) of his client. Human psyches can "contaminate" one another just as physical bodies do. It is no wonder that there exist many tales of the hazards of being a healer. In his autobiography Jung describes how his personal physician died shortly after bringing Jung back to life following a heart attack.[14] In Jewish literature there are also examples of healers who heal others at the cost of their own well-being. The *Sefer Chasidim*, for instance, contains the story of a sick man who had a dream predicting his imminent death. A dream interpreter offered to purchase the dream for a fee. As soon as the transaction took place, the dreamer became healthy—and the dream interpreter died.

The Problem of the Fee

The issue of payment for the services of a professional dream interpreter is worth considering in the context of vocational hazards. The notion of charging a fee for dream interpretation is at least as old as the Greeks. In the temples of Asclepius, one paid a fee after the cure had been effected. Meier notes:

> Apparently the patient had no further obligation after recording the [healing] dream apart from certain thank offerings and the payment of the fee. People gave what they could, in proportion to their wealth. Asclepius often required a literary production of some kind as a thank offering—a paean, for example. Thus he became the patron of cultured and learned men and of artists. . . .
>
> The thank offerings . . . could be paid at anytime within a year. Cases are on record, however, where the god gave those who were too slow in paying their debts a sharp lesson by promptly sending a relapse. This was of course a great cause of scandal to the Early Fathers, who pointed out that the Christian martyrs such as Cosmas and Damian, Cyrus and John, worked their miracle cures . . . free of charge.[15]

The important point emphasize here is that the fee is part of the therapy. Failure to pay the fee is bad for both therapist and patient. The Talmud describes the following incident.

> Bar Hedya was an interpreter of dreams. To one who paid him he used to give a favourable interpretation and to one who did not pay him he gave an unfavourable interpretation. Abaye and Rabbah each had a dream. Abaye gave him a *zuz*, and Rabbah did not give him anything. They said to him: In our dream we had to read the verse, Thine ox shall be slain before thine eyes (Deut. 28:31), etc. To Rabbah he said: Your business will be a failure, and you will be so grieved that you will have no ap-

> petite to eat. To Abaye he said: Your business will prosper, and you will not be able to eat from sheer joy. They then said to him: We had to read in dream the verse, Thou shalt beget sons and daughters but they shall not be thine (Deut. 28:41), etc. To Rabbah he interpreted it in its [literal] unfavourable sense. To Abaye he said: You have numerous sons and daughters, and your daughters will be married and go away, and it will seem to you as if they have gone into captivity. . . .
>
> Finally Rabbah went and gave him a fee. He said to him: I saw a wall fall down. He replied: You will acquire wealth without end. He said: I dreamt that Abaye's villa fell in and the dust of it covered me. He replied to him: Abaye will die and [the presidency of] his College will be offered to you. He said to him: I saw my own villa fall in and everyone came back and took a brick. He said to him: Your teachings will be disseminated throughout the world. He said to him: I dreamt that my head was split open and my brains fell out. He replied: The stuffing will fall out of your pillow. . . .[16]

From this we might derive the insight that a patient in analysis who does not pay the fee may be sabatoging his own therapy, since a resentful analyst is unlikely to act in the patient's best interest. Moreover, the patient who gives a fair exchange for the services received is more likely to value the treatment and invest his own energy in the cure.

Analysts who depend on their fees for their livelihood should carefully consider their financial needs before undertaking to treat no-fee or low-fee patients. If an analyst finds that he is especially hard on no-fee patients, interpreting their dreams in a negative way, it is time for him to take a fresh look at his own money complex. If this cannot be resolved, as when the analyst is either too neurotic or suffering from too much financial hardship, then it may be advisable to terminate the analysis with an appropriate explanation, rather than become a destructive analyst—what Almoli calls "an enemy in revenge."

5. The Art of Positive Dream Interpretation

Throughout the Jewish literature on dreams, one encounters the notion of turning a bad dream to good. Numerous rituals are prescribed for this process, such as fasting for two consecutive days or incanting prayers in front of three people. The focus on bad dreams suggests that the Jews saw dreams primarily as negative forecasts. Although "good omen" dreams do exist, dreams do not usually give us a pat on the back to remind us of our good works and great accomplishments. Instead, they usually offer a self-reflection indicating that we are not living right in some area of our lives or that we are heading for some kind of trouble. For Almoli, the essential purpose of such dreams was to direct the dreamer's energies into action that would reverse the bad omen. Thus, although a dream might be termed negative, the forecast is never carved in stone and is open to transformation into a positive outcome. It is the task of the dream interpreter to find the positive potential in the dream and help make it a reality.

Positive feedback is one of the most powerful tools of any healer. To offer encouragement and recognition by saying, for example, "You are looking better," or "You're moving in the right direction," can have an energizing effect on a person. The healer must reinforce the positive side of people as well as help them to control their negative behavioral patterns.

Negative or critical feedback can be useful in the healing process, but it must be given sparingly and wisely. The growth process always begins wherever a person happens to be; thus, part of the healer's role is to accept the patient as he or she is in the moment. This is the unconditional acceptance that all patients in psychotherapy are entitled to. However, as soon as the person embarks on a journey of growth, the rules are modified and new burdens are placed on him or her. "Know thyself" takes on a new dimension so as to include "Change thyself." Changing old patterns requires the ability to hear some negative feedback and to act on it.

There are some patients who find any negative feedback intolerable. These are often narcissistic individuals who arrive in therapy with a total lack of self-awareness. They are hyperaware of their suffering but have no sense of responsibility for their predicament. I sometimes think of these patients as suffering from "the Rolling Stone syndrome": they're always singing, "I can't get no satisfaction." Why are their wives and husbands having affairs, or why are they failures in their work, or why are they rejected by their children, or why are they alone without a spouse or friends? They have no idea. Until people are able to see how their own behavior brings about their dissatisfaction, they cannot learn to act in a way that will help fulfill their needs.

The Danger of Negative Forecasting

The destructive influence of negative suggestion has been demonstrated by studies of societies in which black magic is practiced. Frequently a person who is told that a witch's curse has been put on him will actually die, apparently from the sheer power of his belief in the efficacy of the curse. Telling someone that he will die in the near future can lead to a self-fulfilling prophecy whereby the person may even bring about his own death.

The Jewish sages had a profound awareness of this danger, especially in the case of dreams interpreted as omens of impending doom. In a passage cited by Almoli (see page 51), the students of a rabbi interpreted a woman's dream in the rabbi's absence, saying, "You will bury your husband." When the woman's husband did in fact die, the rabbi accused his students, "You have murdered the man," reprimanding them with the biblical passage "It came to pass as he [Joseph] interpreted it to us." Almoli comments that since the woman believed that her husband would die no matter what, she may have done nothing to prevent his death; moreover, the husband may have lost his will to live after hearing of the prediction. If the students had used Almoli's positive method of dream interpretation, they would have told the woman, "That is what the dream predicts, but you must go to God and beseech Him to remove the evil from you."

The role of the dream interpreter is to give people hope and help them to live, not prepare them for death. This is not to say that dreams never serve to prepare the dreamer for death, as for example when the dreamer is suffering from a terminal illness or is at an advanced age. Jung observed that the dreams of old people often seemed to indicate that they would live forever—perhaps as a way of affirming to the dreamer the reality of the soul's immortality. Such dreams, however, are not the typical dreams brought to the interpreter.

A modern version of negative interpretation may be seen in the following incident related by Jung.

> An acquaintance of mine once told me a dream in which he stepped out into space from the top of the mountain. I explained to him something of the influence of the unconscious and warned him against dangerous mountaineering expeditions, for which he had a regular passion. But he laughed at such ideas. A few months later while climbing a mountain he actually did step off into space and was killed.[1]

In another version of this story, Jung relates:

> A colleague of mine . . . always teased me about my dream interpretations. Well, I met him one day in the street and he called out to me, "How are things going? Still interpreting dreams? By the way, I've had another idiotic dream. Does that mean something too?" This is what he dreamed: "I am climbing a high mountain, over steep snow covered slopes. I climb higher and higher and it is marvelous weather. The higher I climb the better I feel. I think, "If only I could go on climbing

> like this for ever!" When I reach the summit my happiness and elation are so great that I feel I could mount right up into space. And I discover that I can actually do so: I mount upwards on empty air, and awake in sheer ecstasy." After some discussion, I said, "My dear fellow, I know you can't give up mountaineering, but let me implore you not to go alone from now on. When you go, take two guides, and promise on your word of honor to follow them absolutely." "Incorrigible!" he replied laughing and waved goodbye . . . Two months later . . . when out alone, he was buried by an avalanche, but was dug out in the nick of time by a military patrol that happened to be passing. Three months afterwards . . . he went on a climb with a younger friend, but without guides. A guide standing below saw him literally step out into the air while descending a rock face. He fell on the head of his friend, who was waiting lower down, and both were dashed to pieces far below. That was ecstasis with a vengeance.[2]

In a third account Jung stated that the man was "inextricably involved in a number of shady affairs."[3] And in a fourth account he offered some more personal information. The man was about fifty years of age and told Jung very emphatically that he would never give up his mountain climbing because he had to go to the mountains in order to get away from the city and his family. "This sticking at home does not suit me," he said. "Also he seemed disgusted with his professional work," Jung wrote.

> It occurred to me that his uncanny passion for the mountains must be an avenue of escape from an existence that had become intolerable to him. . . . I told him quite frankly what I thought, namely that he was seeking his death in the mountains, and that with such an attitude he stood a remarkably good chance of finding it. "But that is absurd," he replied, laughing. "On the contrary, I am seeking my health in the mountains."[4]

The way that Jung elaborates the details of this encounter makes me wonder about the appropriateness of his morbid prediction for this poor soul. Jung openly stated that his colleague would die if he continued to mountain-climb. But since the man had made it clear that he would not renounce his passion for the mountains, Jung's forecast may have functioned as a negative suggestion that reinforced the man's self-destructive tendency.

In reading Jung's various versions of this encounter, I was reminded of the warning in the Zohar that you should tell your dream only to a close friend—that is to someone who loves you. One can seriously question whether Jung had a very positive feeling for the man. In one of his accounts, we find the man mocking Jung's preoccupation with the study of dreams. Jung's gloomy interpretation may have been influenced by his negative countertransference toward the man. A dream interpreter who does not like his client would be wise to refer that person to another interpreter.

How might a Jewish interpreter such as Almoli have handled this situation? My fantasy is that Almoli would have searched the dream for some positive solution to the man's self-destructive impulses. In my own experience, dreams in which a person is seeking to climb higher and higher do not necessarily reflect a suicidal wish; rather, they tend to indicate an inflated approach to life. Such dreams could also reflect the desire to get somewhere in the world without the necessary work or the grounding needed for psychological development. In these cases, the task of the psychotherapist–dream interpreter lies in rechanneling the patient's energies into more grounded, "real life" activities in order to restore balance to his or her life.

I once worked with a man who was damaged from years of experimenting with LSD. He reported the following dream:

> I am climbing on this ladder. The ladder separates from the wall. I look up and want to climb higher and higher.

I took this dream as a reflection from his unconscious of his relationship to his inner ladder—that is, the psychological and emotional foundation upon which he had built his existence. His unconscious was telling him through a metaphorical image that his personality structure was in danger. The message, by implication, was that rather than climb higher on this ladder, the dreamer must return to the ground floor or even the foundation or cornerstone of his existence. His unconscious was pointing him toward the need for grounding. The dreamer had lost his connection to the core of his being and was prematurely dwelling among the gods in his desire for higher and higher ungrounded, drug-based experiences. If we compare this man's ladder dream to the biblical dream of Jacob, we can see a marked contrast. Jacob dreams of a solid and secure ladder:

> And he dreamed, and behold a ladder was set upon the earth, and the top of it reached to heaven, and behold the angels of God were ascending and descending on it. (Gen. 28:12)

The Bible's message seems to be clear: if you plan to ascend to God, make sure you have a good ladder and a good foundation.

With some dreams of rising higher, the dream ego may mistake the dream for an ecstatic mystical experience when in fact that is exactly the opposite of the higher self's intention. The intention of these dreams is often to inform the dreamer of his need for more grounding. An example of this was a dream of a man in his late thirties, presented in a Boston dream group:

> I'm driving in a VW that is open at the top, and it is an old car. I am with a friend and we are driving in third gear up a very steep hill. I point to my friend and say, "Look at this—the car is driving so quickly, and in third gear." As I am driving up the hill, a green snake appears, and I gleefully try to run it over, though I am not sure if I have succeeded. I finally reach the top of the hill, and it is like paradise. Everything is this beautiful white. I notice a leaf and a bird that look exactly alike. I show it to my friend, who is unimpressed and responds, "The air is very nice up here." But I was more impressed with what I saw. I awoke feeling that this was the greatest experience of my life, and that it was a positive dream.

In my opinion this is clearly a warning dream. If we look at the dream in its entirety, we note that he is driving his old car in the wrong gear for a steep hill. He then gleefully tries to run down the green snake—a positive figure in the psyche. Imagine how the snake must feel being irrationally chased by some insane driver. He then seems to get stuck in a lofty place with no green around, only a deathly white. The friend could be representative of the side of the dreamer that is aware of the dangerous situation. This dream was reflecting the dreamer's inability to evaluate the self-destructive lifestyle he was leading. He was the kind of person who prided himself on the absence of "green" in his life, and he told the other members of the dream group how he did not have a green thumb and that all of his plants would die. The entire group's agreement on the warning signs in this dream failed to make an impression on the dreamer, who was convinced that his dream was a mystical experience to be savored.

There is a principle in Judaism that you should not rebuke someone who will not heed the rebuke. If, for example, you caution someone against committing a sin, but he ignores you and sins anyway, then you are as guilty of the sin as he is. Applied to the realm of psychotherapy, this principle emphasizes the importance of offering advice in a way that the other person can receive. For the interpreter to tell a person that, based on his dream, he seems to be on the wrong road is painful for both parties. With a negative interpretation, one runs the risk that the dreamer will identify with his negative side, thus inhibiting any positive change or growth. Although it is desirable to become conscious of the dark side of one's personality, there is always the possibility of falling into the darkness, never to surface into the light. The dream interpreter must be aware of the power of his suggestions in the therapeutic relationship.[5] The interpreter's responsibility is an ethical one.

A Two-Step Process

Positive dream interpretation entails a two-step process. The first step is to help the dreamer understand his current predicament as reflected in the dream. The second step involves discovering the remedy or solution to the problem, or what could be called the "action plan." This plan may be suggested explicitly by the dream itself, or it may be elicited from the dreamer in the course of talking with the interpreter.

The recognition of the problem lays the foundation for the solution. A person who is aware of his or her neurosis or illness in a position to benefit from working with a healer. One example is a patient of mine who was continually wasting an inordinate amount of energy in compulsive sexual behavior. One night he dreamed that he was diagnosed as having a "love illness." Through our discussion of the dream, he understood that he was pursuing sexual relationships in order to feel loved. He was then open to exploring other, less destructive activities that might help him to feel loved.

Dreams usually mirror either the conscious or the unconscious situation of the dreamer. The interpreter begins his work by reflecting back to the dreamer the dreamer's own awareness of the problematic situation. In a way, the interpreter is simply telling the dreamer something that he already knows.

The realization that dreamwork—and psychotherapy in general—entails telling people what they already know came to me in a dream of my own. At the time, I was critically reviewing my style of offering dream interpretations. I saw myself stupidly repeating basic commonsense advice to all my patients. Recalling Benjamin Franklin's assertion that "commonsense ain't so common" didn't completely console me. I wanted to be able to give people insights of profound wisdom. Then I had a dream that proclaimed a golden rule of dream analysis: Tell the dreamer only what he already knows. This insight contrasts with the Jungian notion that it is always important to find something *new* in a dream. I had long doubted that theory, and the dream affirmed my unconscious mind's rejection of it. The unconscious has the right and privilege of repeating itself if it feels that a dream message needs to be reemphasized.

Most people seen in therapy have a huge storehouse of wisdom that they fail to act upon. They go to a therapist in order to hear the insights of their own minds and hearts emerge in the context of a dialogue with another human being. I have learned that it is not essential for me to come up with profound and novel insights; what is important is to accompany my patients on their journey of discovering their own inner source of guidance.

A conversation that I once had with a Jungian colleague of mine gave me the opportunity to demonstrate my two-step process. This man, whom I will call David, had been on a whirlwind lecture tour. He had spent a week visiting me in Boston and was now ready to return home. We were at the airport four hours before his scheduled flight, as he was typically anxious and compulsive about everything that he did. David, who suffered from what Fritz Perls called "catastrophic expectations," was enumerating to me all of the possible disasters that could strike at any moment, ranging from missed flights and automobile breakdowns to illness, disability, and impoverishment. He was a pessimist par excellence. I replied that I have basically lived my life with the confidence that I would not get sick or be incapacitated for the rest of my days. I told him that I thought he was obsessively exaggerating his chance of losing everything and that it might be time for him to consider whether there were some areas in his life in which he could reduce his anxiety level.

During the conversation, the difference in our respective dream theories came up. I elaborated on my conviction, based on Jewish sources, that dream interpretation should be a positive and practical way of dealing with a variety of life problems. This approach contrasted with David's own style of interpreting, which regarded dreams as a manifestation of the unconscious without direct relevance to the concerns of conscious life. I described my view of dreams as the voice of the inner healer and explained that the process of interpretation consisted of a diagnosis and a treatment plan. We discussed the biblical story in which Joseph not only gave Pharaoh a interpretation that forecast a famine in Egypt but also advised him to take a practical action in order to transform the negative forecast into a positive outcome.

As a test of my positive approach, my colleague told me a

disturbing dream that he had the night before. In it he was back home, although the dream house didn't look like his actual house and the wife there was not his real wife. The entire house was messy and dirty. He awoke feeling very anxious.

David began the interpretation process by relating that he felt that his anima—the feminine side of his psyche—had made his life too cluttered and messy. His associations continued in this vein, and he observed that he had allowed certain people to abuse his friendship, to the detriment of his family life. David realized that he ought to say no to people who asked to have lunch with him when he really did not want to have lunch with them. Because of his habit of being too generous and agreeable, he had many relationships in which he gave more than he received. He also felt that he had been seeing too many patients each day, with the result that he felt exhausted at night.

After listening to all this, I reminded David that in my method of dream analysis, his understanding of the dream was only the first step; the question still remained, "What are you going to do now?" David acknowledged that the dream was stimulating him to think about how he might clean up the mess of his mismanaged life. He began questioning why he had rushed to the airport four hours before his flight. His image of a worst-case scenario, in which missing the flight would spell disaster, he now realized was an exaggeration. In fact, missing the flight would simply mean buying a new ticket—an expense that was well within his means. It then occurred to him that since the ticket was being paid for by the organization sponsoring his lectures, why didn't he fly first class? This thought in turn led him to reevaluate his practice of going on lecture tours. He acknowledged that flying around the world to give lectures was no longer worthwhile to him. He resolved to travel primarily for pleasure and to curtail his business travel severely. He also realized that he did not need to have others pay for his trips; he could travel when and where he liked at his own expense and need not be restricted by unrealistic fears of poverty, mishaps, and loss.

In summary, David's dream can be seen as a communication

from his inner healer to his ego about the irrational manner in which he was creating stress and anxiety for himself and his family. As soon as he was willing to look at the dream in this way, his own innate problem-solving abilities were constellated, and he discovered that he could take his life into his own hands and start managing it more wisely.

The Next Step: The Action Plan

Once the message of the dream has been understood and the solution has been determined, the next step is to take the appropriate corrective action. This is what Almoli calls the "fulfillment" of the dream.

The fulfillment of the dream is clearly up to the dreamer. However, Almoli emphasizes the need to receive the correct interpretation in order for the dream to be fulfilled. He cites the kabbalistic assertion that people should only tell their dreams to a close friend, explaining that an interpreter who does not have the dreamer's best interests at heart is likely to give a wrong or negative interpretation. As a result, the dreamer may exhaust his resources in futile efforts. If one wastes energy pursuing false goals, the real intent of the dream will fail to be actualized. As a Jewish proverb declares, you cannot dance simultaneously at two weddings.

The interpreter must search the dream for clues to the next step, what the dreamer should be doing right now. Most of the people who consult a psychotherapist have gotten derailed in their lives and need to go back on track. Often their predicament is a consequence of having failed to act out the appropriate next step in their development.

The purpose of life is to achieve one's potential in every area of existence. An individual who stops developing may fall into a depression, exhibit some psychosomatic or neurotic symptom, indulge in addictive or compulsive behavior, or even have a psychotic breakdown. Among the more severely ill people, the sense of losing control of their destiny had gone far beyond the more common neurotic state of being. Such disturbed individuals usually do not consult a psychotherapist, because they are too disoriented to realize that they have a problem and need professional help. I have often defined insanity as the condition of believing that one is sane. Although dream interpretation can be helpful for this group as well, the degree of pathology may inhibit these people from developing a therapeutic alliance with the psychotherapist, the trust and confidence in the healer that is a prerequisite for any healing ritual.

Jung recognized the link between mental health and fulfilling one's destiny. Part of his work with patients was to evaluate the basis of their existence: What were they living for? What gave their lives meaning? Why did they experience a loss of meaning in their lives? Jung's attitude toward charting the course of life was essentially conservative. He believed in the individual's basic responsibility to humanity, country, family, and self. He wrote:

> One of the most important things to consider is the age of the individual; that should make a tremendous difference in our attitude when we analyse. Everything that is important in the latter part of life may be utterly negligible in the early part of life. The next consideration should be whether the individual has accomplished an adaptation to life, whether he is above or below the standard level of life and whether he has fulfilled the reasonable expectations. At forty, one should have roots, a position, family, etc., and not be psychologically adrift. People who have not married, who are not established in life, have the psychology of the nomad, in no man's land. Such people have a different goal from those firmly established in homes and families, for that task is still to be accomplished. The question to be asked is, is the individual normally adapted or not?[6]

I am reminded of man of thirty-nine who spent better part of his energies lusting after eighteen-year-old women. He had been married for ten years but had postponed having children, although his wife felt strongly that her biological clock was sending out alarms concerning her childless state. He rationalized that he was still developing his career as an artist and that he was in no position to start a family. This man had numerous dreams of death, and I realized that his dreams were confronting him with his mortality. The thought flashed through my mind that here was a person who was three-quarters dead and still living like a teenager in love! This man needed his dreams to help him change the direction of his life and begin embarking on the basic tasks of his species.

In my own dream life, the motif of finding extra rooms in my home has usually symbolized the need to continue on my own search for development. I often dream of rooms in the attic or of finding wings of the upper floors that I never knew existed. Symbolically, the upper floors of the house represent the head, or the intellect, so that my dreams of the top floors suggest a need to develop the thinking side of my psyche. Sometimes I dream of discovering new wings on the ground floor, which I take to mean that my relationship to my body, work, or family—the ground of my earthly existence—is in need of discovery and development. Dreams lend themselves to the fantasy of discovery: the messages of the dream are like multifaceted diamonds embedded in mud, waiting to be discovered. I think of dreams as important clues in the lifelong treasure hunt for meaning and contentment.

A Sense of the Future

I have been struck by how many of my patients live without a sense of the future. Not only are they out of touch with their mortality, but they have no concept of life as a long-term project requiring goal setting, planning, and decision making. Today there is widespread appreciation in Western culture of the Eastern emphasis on awareness of the present moment—"Be here now." By contrast, our own culture stresses the need for contact with the future in order to manage one's life effectively. People with no sense of the future often end up in psychotherapy because they feel out of control, like ships in a storm without a helmsman. They typically have an egocentric attitude toward life, as if the world were designed for them alone. They are unable to assume responsibilities for other human beings and find it difficult to form long-term intimate relationships. I have worked with numerous men and women who trade in their relationships more frequently than they trade in their cars, and who suffer the consequences of their choices.

Henry came into analysis because of a crisis stemming from this kind of orientation toward life. He and his wife were living as free as birds, without the burden of a nest. They had an open marriage, each indulging in affairs without much guilt, traveled extensively, and had money in the bank. I concluded that Henry had adopted this lifestyle at the expense of a normal family. The individual who chooses not to have children is missing one of the basic components of what it means to be human. It is of course one's freedom to choose, but then one is also free to choose most other forms of self-destructive behavior. Analyzing the decision not to reproduce oneself often uncovers a fountain of repressed rage whose source lies in early childhood. Because of this rage, the individual refuses to offer back to life what life has given to him. It is as if he were saying, "Aren't I enough for this world?"

One of Henry's dreams was about a local store called Lechmere. I interpreted the dream as a message from his unconscious that he was living like a "mere leech," taking from life without giving back. Henry strongly resisted this interpretation and accused me of forcing my narrow philosophy of life on him. I realized that many of the things I was saying to him were the same words he had heard from his own parents. Indeed, psychotherapy typically provides the patient with reparenting or surrogate parenting. The benefit of advising people through dream interpretation is that the primary source of insight comes from the dreamer's own psyche rather than the psychotherapist's bias. In Henry's case, he was living a life with no foundation in civilization, and this was not acceptable to his higher self.

The Inner Advisor

The dream itself is the dreamer's personal advisor, or what I call the voice of the inner healer. In the words of Albert Schweitzer, "Each patient carries his own doctor inside him. They come to us not knowing that truth. We are at our best when we give the doctor who resides within each patient a chance to go to work."[7] I have often had the experience of discussing with a patient his or her problems of the moment and their possible solution, only to find that the person has already had a dream that clearly points the way.

An example is Christina, who had come to discuss the problems she was having with her husband. Trained as a Jungian analyst, she had diagnosed him as a functioning alcoholic who was not achieving his full potential because of his dependency. In our discussion, I pointed out that her occasional use of prescribed tranquilizers was similar to her husband's use of alcohol. I explained that for many individuals drinking is a form of self-medication, and there was no guarantee that things would get better if her husband stopped taking his "medicine"; indeed, they could even become worse. This being the case, it might be unwise for her to get so upset over her husband's condition. He was basically dancing as fast as he could, and his alcohol use had not resulted in physical abuse of her or the children, driving while intoxicated, or a serious disruption of his career.

Our discussion centered on my feeling that she was being too critical toward her husband, which had the effect of lowering his self-esteem; he would then turn to drinking as a way of restoring his damaged self-image. I also felt that she was overdependent on him to meet all of the family's financial needs. After all, she had the potential of increasing her own earning power as a social worker. My basic advice to Christina was "Stop protesting and do more yourself."

The other problem we discussed was that her husband might be masochistically requesting her to punish him for his drinking; but that did not mean that she had to accede to his wish. Criticizing a spouse for recurring minor infringements can be very draining for the one who is always wielding the whip. In addition, the admonisher has to deal with the spouse's anger at being punished.

After this discussion, Christina presented her dream of a demonstration at which a sniper is taking shots at the protesters. The motif of a protester having to deal with the aggression of a sniper seemed clearly to refer to what we had just discussed. In the next segment of the dream, she finds herself in a medieval castle. She notices the guard gate and sees that the interior of the castle is very sooty. The problem of being one's mate's guard is that it is a very dirty job. The idea of entering the sooty place may also reflect her need to get her hands dirty in the world of work and stop being totally dependent on her husband's career.

Finally, Christina reported, "The Pope started coming toward me from the direction of the guards. At first I panicked. Then as a last resort I took the offensive and said, 'You can kiss my hand.' This shocked him momentarily, and I was out of trouble." In this final segment of the dream, we see the new attitude that is needed to solve the problem. Christina rebels against the traditional patriarchal authority symbolized by the Pope, and instead of kissing the Pope's hand, she says to him, "You can kiss my hand," which was like telling the Pope, "You can kiss my ass." The attitude that would lead to Christina's transformation would be one of greater independence, rather than an adaptation to life based on being dependent. She must become her own Pope.

Looking for Love

While some patients in analysis are unable to set goals appropriate to their developmental stage, others are disheartened by their anguish over failing to achieve such goals. The issue of finding a husband and having children probably drives more women into therapy than any other problem. For some of these women, an abortion undergone earlier adds tremendous suffering to their plight. An unmarried, childless woman of forty who had an abortion when she was younger will often dream of the aborted baby growing older in successive dreams, as if the child were living on in the interior world.

Among the women in my practice who are disappointed over their lack of an intimate relationship, dreams will often draw their attention to aspects of their personality that are counter-productive to their goal and also contrary to their self-image. These are neglected, unconscious sides of the person that the higher self presents in a dream for the ego's consideration. The unconscious uses the technique of "Imagine you are someone else" to introduce a more productive self-image to the dreamer.

Rachel was thirty-nine and had never been married when she dreamed of finding three pairs of miniature shoes in a little plastic bubble of the kind one gets from vending machines. She tried the tiny shoes on, and to her amazement they fit.

Rachel was five foot nine and had always felt uncomfortable with anyone but a very tall man. Although her feeling was understandable, as a criterion for choosing a partner it had become too limiting. In her dream, with its Cinderella motif, she was shown a new self-image to adopt: that of a small, dainty person. This would open up the field of men she found attractive to a larger group than before, which could increase her chances of finding a satisfying relationship. Her dream also seemed to carry the voice of optimism, confronting the depressed, pessimistic dreamer with a new, positive attitude.

Many people limit their potential for relationships by adopting unrealistic standards. One woman who was nearing fifty refused even to consider men who showed signs of age such as balding or loose skin. She insisted on maintaining her aversion to any man whose body did not conform to the fantasy of a handsome, muscular youth. Her recurring dreams of not being able to find a place to make love helped her eventually to see that her attitude was inhibiting the possibility of finding love with a real human being.

Another woman whom I treated was struggling with forming a long-term relationship without much success until she had the following "proclamation" dream: she heard a voice state emphatically, "*Don't turn lovers into friends!*" This woman had remained close friends with all of her former lovers, men who had rejected her as a marriage partner. She told me that she used to say farewell to a lover who had just broken up with her by making love to him. Her unconscious had probably attempted to communicate the need for her to change her style, but her ego did not awaken to this insight until the dream confronted her with a "Now hear this" statement.

Another woman, age thirty-seven, who seemed never to be sufficiently satisfied with a man to tie the knot, dreamed that Cary Grant called her up for a date. She said, "Cary, I'm sorry, but no." A voice was then heard proclaiming: "Mary, if not him, who?" This challenge from her unconscious humorously brought home the message that she needed to reexamine her standards for matrimonial eligibility.

In general I find that dreams have a sense of relevance in presenting themes that are pertinent to the dreamer's current needs. Dreams rarely regurgitate personal history, except in case of post-traumatic stress disorder, in which the dreamer relives a traumatic event such as combat in war. As a rule, what we already have, we do not dream of getting. Thus, people who are already in a loving relationship usually don't dream about erotic encounters with their partners. Dreams bring us into contact with what we don't have or what we need to acquire.

An example of how dreams can help restore the balance in a person's lifestyle is the case of Judah, a very successful businessman whose personal life was impoverished. His career goals dominated his life, and his compulsive work habits left no time or energy for deep relationships. He had lost contact with his friends over the years, he was oblivious to the needs of a woman with whom he was having an exploitative extramarital affair, and his relationship with his wife was almost nonexistent. All of the dreams that Judah reported to me featured cameo appearances of his neglected friends of the past. The specific content of these dreams seemed less important than the obvious theme that his unconscious was repeatedly drumming into his consciousness: friend, friends, friends! Gradually he was maneuvered into recognizing his need for a more balanced life with more intimate relationships. Not only was this good for his own happiness and wholeness, but it also helped him focus on the impact he was having on significant others in his life. Judah's dreams guided him toward the difficult but necessary task of reorienting himself away from being exclusively self-absorbed and toward an awareness of the pain he had caused to both his lover and his wife.

Mirroring the Self

Many dreams have the function of mirroring the self in a way that confronts us with the way we *are* rather than the way we wish we were.

Some examples of this function appeared in the dreams of Alice, who experienced life as a continuous chain of traumatic incidents. Her cars and her boyfriends were always lemons, and "How could I know?" was her trademark excuse. At first she considered herself the innocent victim of circumstances or bad luck, but slowly she realized that she had some of the classic traits of adult children of alcoholics, who take on the role of caretaker of humanity while their own existence remains in a chronic state of despair. Alice dreamed:

> I am on the street, and I observe how one car forces another car into a ditch and then drives off. I go over to the victim and offer my services to him as witness, since I had observed the whole proceeding. He declines my offer. I go off in a huff, as I cannot understand why he would not want my service as witness, since what I had observed was in his interest in dealing with the insurance company.

In this dream, the masculine side of her personality, which may be dealing here with time management, is clearly telling her feminine nurturing side, "Don't waste your time, lady. If you want to nurture, why don't you focus on your own undernourished, mismanaged existence?" In other words, mind your own business! I was reminded of the talmudic notion of putting your own house in order before setting out to help others.

Another dream image that Alice reported was, "I am in the rafters." Here her unconscious was desperately trying to communicate to her the need to have her feet on the ground. To be a saint in the service of others, one must first be grounded in one's own life and in the purpose of one's being.

People often seek out a psychotherapist because of problems related to their depressed or inflated self-image. Self-image is the cornerstone of mental health, and Jung, observing the relationship between opposite forces within the psyche, noted that contrasting self-images often coexist in a personality as two sides of the same coin. People who are depressed in their conscious life often harbor in their unconscious an inflated image of their innate gifts and potential powers and what they imagine should have been their just fate. We might say that inside the depressed person, an inflated little Napoleon is struggling to get out. Similarly, the megalomaniac often harbors a deep-rooted feeling of worthlessness in the unconscious.

In order for such personalities to heal, the prideful person must establish contact with his unconscious depression, and the depressed individual needs to be more in contact with his Napoleonic optimism. Dreams will often confront us with whatever sides of our personality we are repressing or with our "unlived" life." They represent our desire to be whole people, whenever this wholeness is beneficial. I see the goal of the dream-maker as assisting people in the recognition, assimilation, and balancing of all one's personality components. Jung saw these components—which he called complexes, emotionally charged clusters of ideas, images, memories, and feelings—as being acted out by the characters in our dreams. I have often envisioned the dream as conducting a form of group therapy for the complexes. Our various complexes are the dream's initial audience, and in comparison to the few dreams that we recall in the morning, our psyche and its components witness many inner dramas during the night.

Bob was a depressed person who was unaware that deep in his unconscious he harbored an inflated self-image. In his conscious life, he felt like the helpless victim of his wife, his bosses, and the world at large. This feeling of helplessness was reflected in dreams such as one in which he is on an athletic team but finds himself watching the game from the sidelines without even being in uniform.

But other sides of his personality also came out in dreams. In one dream, he found himself driving an eighteen-wheel truck down the entire East Coast, going from on-ramps to highways to cities. The context of this dream was that business had dried up for Bob and he was feeling depressed. But an analysis of his business problem made it clear that in order to turn this situation around, he had to leave the safety of waiting in his office for new accounts and go out into the world to generate some business. Bob was harboring delusional feelings of grandeur in expecting business to come to him unsolicited, and his unconscious presented him with the solution to his problem: he was to identify more with his inner trucker, go out into the world, and find his fortune by way of hard work, rather than waiting for his deserved salvation.

In another dream that same week, he was in the basement with a former business associate who had moved to the West Coast. This associate symbolized his need to be geographically mobile in order to explore new accounts in other parts of the country. Bob realized that it was time for him to become bolder and more expansive in his search for new business. Both dreams presented him with alternative modes of reflection and action.

Judaism has its own perspective on what today is popularly known as a superiority complex or an arrogant personality. People with this characteristic are seen as indulging in the sin of pride. They fail to develop a lifestyle and self-image based on the divine plan for all of humanity and an awareness of the shared frailties of human beings. These individuals live as if there were no Designer, Creator, or Planner in the universe. A classic example is the biblical figure of Nebuchadnezzar, whose inflationary self-aggrandizement is diagnosed by the prophet Daniel after hearing the king's dream:

> I saw, and behold a tree in the midst of the earth, and the height thereof was great. The tree grew and was strong, and the height thereof reached unto heaven, and the sight thereof to the end of all the earth. The leaves thereof were fair, and the fruit thereof much, and in it was food for all; the beasts of the field had shadow under it, and the fowls of the heaven dwelt in the branches thereof, and all flesh was fed of it. I saw in the visions of my head upon my bed, and, behold, a watcher and a holy one came down from heaven. He cried aloud, and said thus: Hew down the tree, and cut off its branches, shake off its leaves, and scatter its fruit; let the beasts get away from under it, and the fowls from its branches. Nevertheless leave the stump of its roots in the earth, even in a band of iron and brass, in the tender grass of the field; and let it be wet with the dew of heaven, and let his portion be with the beasts in the grass of the earth; let his heart be changed from man's, and let a beast's heart be given unto him; and let seven times pass over him. The matter is by the decree of the watchers, and the sentence by the word of the holy ones; to the intent that the living may know that the Most High rules in the kingdom of men, and gives it to whomsoever He will, and sets up over it the lowest of man. (Dan. 4:7–15)

When a experienced dream interpreter is confronted with a dream like this, he immediately realizes the gravity of the dreamer's personality state. The dream, being a symbolic reflection from the higher self to the ego, is diagnostic by implication. Nebuchadnezzar's dream is clearly the product of a deranged megalomaniac. "Then Daniel . . . was appalled for a while, and his thoughts frightened him." It is alarming to be confronted with such a pathological state, so Daniel needs some time to formulate a strategy for interpreting the dream in a manner that would lead to the king's repentance rather than the loss of Daniel's own head.

Nebuchadnezzar notices Daniel's hesitation, and then Daniel begins his interpretation:

> The tree that you saw . . . it is you, O king. . . . And where the king saw a watcher and a holy one coming down from heaven, and saying: Hew down the tree, and destroy it . . . this is the interpretation, O king, and it is the decree of the Most High, which is come upon my lord the king, that you shall be driven from men, and your dwelling shall be with the beasts of the field, and you shall be made to eat grass as oxen, and shall be wet with the dew of heaven, and seven times shall pass over you, till you know that the Most High rules in the kingdom of men, and gives it to whomsoever He will. . . . Wherefore, O king, let my counsel be acceptable unto you, and break off your sins by almsgiving, and your iniquities by showing mercy to the poor. (Dan. 4:17–25)

Daniel informs Nebuchadnezzar of a basic assumption in dream interpretation: that the parts of the dream are symbolic representations of the life of the dreamer. He explains that the tree is a symbol of the king himself, who has grown too large for a human being. Daniel advises the king to temporarily abandon his palace and live the life of a nomadic beggar, give charity, and become more emphatic toward the poor. Nebuchadnezzar follows Daniel's treatment plan, and when he is well again, he offers the following proclamation:

> And my understanding returned unto me, and I blessed the Most High, and I praised and honored Him that lives forever. . . . Now I Nebuchadnezzar praise and honor the king of heaven; for all his works are truth, and His ways are justice, and those that walk in pride he is able to abase. (Dan. 4:31–34)

The Voice of Conscience

The kinds of problems that people bring to a dream interpreter or psychotherapist today are essentially the same as the problems that people once brought to their religious leaders. Now, however, these problems are addressed within the framework of a doctor-patient relationship. Although psychoanalytic theory evolved out of a medical model, for Jung analysis was a kind of medical ministry, closely connected with religious concerns such as the search for meaning and the importance of morality.

Jung tells of a thirty-year-old man who came to him with voluminous autobiographical material exemplifying his psychoanalytical understanding of his life. Yet despite all his insight, he had not succeeded in curing his neurosis. After taking a careful history of the man, Jung said, "You mention in your autobiography that you often spend the winter in Nice and the summer in St. Moritz. I take it you are the son of wealthy parents?" "Oh no," the man answered, "they are not wealthy at all." "Then no doubt you have made your money yourself?" Again the answer was no. It turned out that he got the money from a thirty-six-year-old schoolteacher who was living austerely while sending him on luxurious vacations in the hope of a future marriage with him. The man, however, had no intention of marrying her. He rejected Jung's suggestion that this situation might be contributing to his neurosis.

After recounting the incident, Jung comments, "He was one of the many who believe that morals have nothing to do with neurosis and that sinning on purpose is not sinning at all, because it can be intellectualized out of existence. . . . With views like his only a criminal can adapt to life."[8] Elsewhere he remarks of the same case, "His want of conscience was the cause of his neurosis, and it is not hard to see why scientific understanding failed to help him. His fundamental error lay in his moral attitude."[9]

I have been struck by the number of dreams that seem to be the voice of the dreamer's moral conscience. A particularly striking dream that I myself had around the time I was first researching Jewish dream interpretation was a horrifying image of Hitler's dead body rotting inside of me. As a rabbi in Germany who occasionally took groups of Jews on visits to death camps like Dachau, I had a tendency to project all the evils of the world onto the Germans. This dream had a humbling and humanizing effect on me. I came to realize that the historical calamity inflicted upon the Jewish people by Germany did not exempt Jews from facing their own character defects. I had to come to terms with my own rage stemming from my early childhood experiences. My dream was informing me of my own anger and aggression.

I happened upon another example during a train ride to Zurich. An elderly German woman boarded the train and, when she noticed that I was reading a book on dream interpretation, struck up a conversation with me. She told me that during the war she had had recurring dreams of heaps of naked bodies piled on top of one another. She tearfully concluded her account by saying, "But how was I to know that this was actually happening?" It occurred to me that in fact her unconscious did know and was trying to communicate it to her in the dream.

Another time while riding the train I met a French businessman who was a survivor of the Holocaust. As our conversation turned to dreams, he informed me that he never dreamed, except after eating certain foods that gave him indigestion. Then he would always have the same dream, in which he was back in his hometown synagogue in Poland. He would be praying fervently with a prayer shawl over his head in the manner of devout Jews. Then the scene would shift and he would find himself in front of the liberal synagogue that he currently attended. He would finally wake up with a headache. His association to these images was that he no longer felt any strong religious feelings in synagogue; it was simply a place where he congregated with his friends and business acquaintances. The dream seemed to be the voice of his conscience, reminding him that he needed to pay more attention to his spiritual life, which had once been so important to him.

In my current practice, many dreams expressing the moral instinct are those of parents in relation to their children. One woman was referred to me because of severe depression and psychosomatic complaints. The initial dream that she presented in therapy was a nightmare in which her baby was being burned in a toaster oven. A year earlier, this woman had decided to relinquish custody of her child to the father, from whom she was divorced. It was clear that her conscience would not let her release this responsibility without a major battle.

A nightmare reported by another patient closely followed her abortion. In the dream she was fighting with her boyfriend when suddenly she saw the skeleton of a baby collapse in front of her. She awoke with the horrified thought, "My God, what have I done to my baby?" The dream elicited powerful guilt feelings, which this woman needed to work through in order to reconsider her values and goals.

Reversal of Fortune

People consult a psychotherapist because for one reason or another life is not working out for them. The typical difficulties presented in therapy fall into the two categories defined by Freud: love and work. I have already mentioned several cases of people whose problems were mainly in the area of relationships. A great many other patients are struggling with work or financial problems.[10]

One should not underestimate financial difficulties as a major contributor to psychological distress. I am reminded of a tragic incident involving a Swiss psychiatrist who suffered from severe depression because his wife was ill with schizophrenia. He had decided to remain married for the children's sake, but eventually he broke down and was committed to a mental hospital, where he took his own life by hanging himself with a shoestring. The symbol of the shoestring reflected his fear that his depressive illness would demolish his life savings.

In my own practice, dreams have often pointed the way to a better financial situation and thus alleviated many stress-related symptoms. Rachel, for example, came into analysis with the belief that her career in special education destined her to a life of hard work and poverty. I refused to accept the picture that she painted of her situation as fixed and hopeless; I thought that her negative belief was functioning as a self-fulfilling prophecy. My work with Rachel consisted of first listening to her tale of woe and then searching her dreams for signs of a transformation.

In one of her dreams, there is an assertive red-haired woman and red-haired man. Rachel is helping to hold a fragile baby but finds it very difficult, as she needs both hands to avoid a collision with a helicopter. The scene shifts to a home where the red-haired couple are discussing some kind of genetic development that they had observed in insects, dogs, and children—all females. It was a mystery they were trying to solve. The redheaded man had a treasure, a collection of beautiful gold, copper, and bronze vessels, on which he was being complimented. When asked how much the collection was worth, he named an enormous sum, and when asked how long he had worked to get it, he replied, "Five hours." It seems he had some special knowledge that he was able to exchange for the treasure.

Rachel had a problem in getting the treasures in life. She undervalued her own knowledge and worth, and lacked the assertive qualities of the red-haired people. The dream implied that if someone were to be justly compensated his or her expertise, five hours of work should pay handsomely. By contrast, Rachel was overworked, underpaid, and not partaking of the rewards of her culture.

Gradually Rachel was able to let go of her negative self-diagnosis, and after a few years she found what she called the only job in the city where a special-education teacher could earn a middle-class income. Soon after landing the job, she found a beautiful house that she could afford to buy with her new salary. She also began to combine her artistic talent with her educational expertise and eventually wrote and illustrated—and published—books in her field. The situation that she had originally labeled as permanent bad luck had reversed.

Reversal of fortune is often not difficult to accomplish. Through a change in jobs, attitudes, or habits, one's financial situation can undergo a dramatic change. One may become more resourceful and thus increase one's earning capacity, or may abandon self-destructive behaviors such as compulsive gambling, addiction to shopping, or throwing money into unnecessary medical procedures.

Sometimes dreams will point out areas that are no longer working or worth investing energy in. A humorous example is this dream of a young woman: "I was a prostitute who was not making any money. A man who I was friendly with told me I should use a paintbrush and I would improve." The dream was instrumental in transforming this woman from a bored housewife into a creative person with a new career that drew on her artistic abilities. Too often, financial failure is the result of a pessimistic self-fulfilling prophecy. If psychotherapy did nothing more than constellate the inner voice of optimism and hope, it would serve a useful purpose.

Dreams can provide the motivating force for many good changes in our lives. The rest, of course, is up to us. As Goethe wrote, "Whatever you can do, or dream you can, begin it. Boldness has genius, power, and magic in it."

6. Dream Incubation

According to the ancient dream theorists, the benefit derived from dreams depends partly on the rituals of preparation for the dream. The need to incubate a dream is based on the supposition that dreams are a channel of divine wisdom and can be especially helpful in personal problem solving.

If the dream is a manifestation of the divine, then the bedtime incantation or prayer sets the stage for the epiphany. This no doubt accounts for the continuous expressions of humility that characterize most ancient dream prayers. These prayers also typically spell out in no uncertain terms the dreamer's expectations from the dream. Since dreams were seen as personal problem solvers, the dream prayer had to be in a flexible form, so that each individual could fill in the blanks with his or her unique situation. Although the ensuing dream was seen as the answer to the dreamer's request, a professional dream interpreter was often required to clarify the answer, for it was accepted that there are times when we receive divine inspiration but fail to understand the communication.

Although the Jewish dream ritual was called *she'elat chalom*, which literally means "dream question," the actual prayers were more concerned with receiving a dream answer to a waking question. As R. J. Werblowsky writes:

> The question was accompanied by the proper formulae, which were then supposed to become effective during sleep. The popularity of the method is borne out by the fact that we possess literally "hundreds of recipes" for it. One such recipe, chosen at random, may illustrate the procedure generally:
> Dream question: write this [Divine] Name on [a piece of] parchment, put it under your head, and thus address the Angel

> of Dreams: I adjure you with the great, mighty, and awesome Name [of God] that you visit me this night and answer my question and request, whether by dream, by vision, by [indicating] a verse from scripture, by speech . . . or by [showing me some] writing, in a manner that I should not forget but remember [on waking] my question and my request [together with the answer]. Amen, Selah.[1]

Another kind of dream request invoked angels and spirits to appear in one's dreams:

> Jacob Halevi, who, it is reported, induced his divinatory dreams by putting himself in a trance, used a simple request: "Oh, supreme king, great, mighty, and revered God, guardian of the covenant and fount of grace for Thy followers, preserve Thy covenant and Thy grace for us, and command Thy holy angels who are appointed over the replies to 'dream questions' to give a true and a proper answer, unqualified and specific, to the question I shall ask before Thy glory," etc. . . . Sometimes the answer came that in heaven itself there was a division of opinion . . . sometimes the first reply that Jacob received was unsatisfactory, so that he had to repeat his question two and three times, insisting upon a clearer response. Certain Biblical selections were also useful toward this end. Ps. 23 and 42, each recited seven times with its "names," were guaranteed to produce dream replies. If one writes Deut. 29:28 and its "names" on his hand and sleeps with that hand under his head the angel of dreams will favor him.[2]

The process of dream incubation generally involves attention to the physical setting of the room in which the dream will take place, the actual ritual of preparing the dream request, preparing one's body and mind to receive the divine communication, and a commitment as to how one will handle the divine gift of the dream once it is received. The intention to record the dream and search for its meaning is usually a basic component of the prayer—just as today, people in Jungian analysis are instructed to record their dreams in a journal upon awakening and to bring them to the analyst.

I found an example of a highly developed dream-question petition in a mystical Jewish encyclopedia first published in 1698. I have translated it in its entirety to demonstrate the various components of the ritual of asking-the-dream:

> Fast for one day [from sundown to sundown]. Upon completion of the fast, purify yourself by going to the *mikveh* [ritual immersion]. That night, refrain from eating meat or drinking wine, and only partake of liquids and fruits like raisins and figs, but not enough to feel full or satisfied. Before retiring, wash your hands. Recite the Shema [bedtime prayer] as usual, and then intone silently the following three verses.
>
> *Recite ten times*:
>
> You make me to know the path of life: in Your presence is fullness of joy, in Your right hand bliss forevermore. (Ps. 16:11)
>
> Lord, You have heard the desire of the humble. You will direct their hearts. You will cause Your ear to attend. (Ps. 10:17)
>
> *Recite ten times*:
>
> He reveals the deep and secret things; He knows what is in the darkness, and the light dwells with Him. (Dan. 2:22)
>
> *Recite three times*:
>
> In the name of God, the God of Israel, the Lord of Hosts, the Good. Show me a good dream.
>
> *Recite three times*:
>
> El, the Lord of Hosts, the Correct. Show me a correct dream.
>
> *Recite three times*:
>
> El, the God of Truth and of Hosts, show me a true dream.
>
> *Recite three times*:
>
> El, the Trustworthy Lord of Hosts, show me a righteous dream.
>
> Amen, Selah, Eternal.
>
> *The following request is recited three times*:
>
> In the Name of God, the Lord of Israel, and the Lord of the earth, El, the Lord of the Spirits, who commands in the heavens and rules below. In seeking a request and finding a solu-

tion, I [state your name], Your servant, son of Your maidservant, come with a supplication and arrive with a humble heart and with a low spirit and short of breath to seek out mercy before Your Glorious Throne, and that this time shall be a time of acceptance, a time of mercy, and a time of listening before You. And You shall surely have mercy, and You shall constellate Your Mercy and Your Kindness upon me [state your name] at this time and during this season, to notify me of all I require in order to understand your response, based upon my petition, which is [state your request], within my night visions, when sleep falls upon me. Do this for the sake of the holiness of Your great Name, and in behalf of the worthiness of Your servants Abraham, Isaac, and Jacob, and to clearly establish this in its simple truth, because only in Your hand is the power and the strength, the counsel and the understanding, I have none other to depend on except You and upon the words of Your Torah. And because of our iniquities the Holy Spirit has left us, and we no longer have prophets or visionaries or the Urim and Tumim to ask of them. Therefore, we have reverted to asking advice from dreams.

And now let my prayer ascend to You and my supplications before You and Your Glorious Throne, El, the Lord of Hosts. And open for me [state your name] the gates and entranceways up above, doors of truth and doors of prophecy, during this night. I should be notified in a language of clear words from the Torah, Prophets, or Writings, in order to know what is essential and necessary for the interpretive reply to my inquiry, which is [state request]. (If the request is for a remedy for illness, one should ask, "What kind of remedy should I [state your name] take? Should it be a substance or an amulet, charm, or something like that?") Answer with a precise response with a well-known verse, clear and clean without any impurities, or in some other manner that will be obvious for me [state your name], so that I will know and understand everything that You tell me; and I will never forget it, because You have revealed secrets and notified me of the hidden through Your great powers and through Your angels, Your holy servants.

Blessed be the name of Your glorious kingdom forever and ever.

Recite Psalm 23 in its entirety three times. Each time the name of the Lord appears, recite the name Shaddai.

Shaddai is my shepherd; I shall not want.
He makes me to lie down in green pastures;
He leads me beside the still waters.
He restores my soul.
He guides me in straight paths for His name's sake.
Yea, though I walk through the valley of the shadow of death,
I will fear no evil.
For You are with me;
Your rod and Your staff, they comfort me,
You prepare a table before me in the presence of my enemies;
You have anointed my head with oil; my cup runs over.
Surely goodness and mercy shall follow me all the days of my life;
And I shall dwell in the house of Shaddai forever.

Recite the following verse seven times normally and seven times backward {in Hebrew}: Now it came to pass in the thirtieth year, in the fourth month, in the fifth day of the month, as I was among the captives by the river Chebar, that the heavens were opened, and I saw visions of God. (Ezek. 1:1)

Recite three times:

For, lo, He that forms the mountains, and created the wind, and declares unto man what is his thought. (Amos 4:13)

Recite three times:

For in You, O Lord, do I hope; You will answer, O Lord my God. (Isa. 2:3)

Recite three times:

For the Lord is a God of knowledge, and by Him actions are weighed. (Ps. 38:10)

Recite three times:

And he dreamed, and behold a ladder was set upon the earth, and the top of it reached to heaven; and behold the angels of God were ascending and descending on it. (Gen. 28:12)

Recite three times:

Into Your hand I commit my spirit; You have redeemed me, O Lord, God of truth. (Ps. 31:6)

Recite three times:

And so may it be pleasing before You, God, my God, and the God of my fathers, that You will send forth Your holy and pure angels Asah, Basah, Gasa, Agaf, Shagaf, and Nagaf, who are appointed over dreams, who will inform me of what I require as a reply to my request, which is [state the request]. And I will never forget it. Amen Selah.

And so I beseech you, the pure and holy angel appointed over dreams, who is Gabriel, the Master of Visions, whose name is the same numerical value as the word for "vision" [246]. We recognize the angels Asah, Basah, Gasa, Agaf, Shagaf, and Nagaf, and those that we don't know about, they should come in peace and not in anger or in anguish. It should be good and not evil and threatening. It should be calm and not terrorizing. It should be open and revelatory and not closed and hidden, in order that I may be informed in my dream what I need to know as a reply to my request, which is [state your request], so that I will understand without any hindrances whatsoever.

Just as you informed Joseph of the interpretations of the dreams of the chief butler and chief bartender and also of Pharaoh, the King of Egypt, and just as you informed Daniel of Nebuchadnezzar's dream and its interpretation, and in other instances as well, inform me with a shining face and peacefully, and not with an angry face. Do not frighten me. And notify me on this night with a clear matter and a honest response, so there will be no hesitation concerning your response to my request, which is [state your request], from the Torah, Prophets, or Writings in the Holy Language with clear expressions and so on. And I will remember and not forget!

All this is in order that El, the God of Truth, will relate a truthful matter, and in order that my God, who is trustworthy, will notify me clarifying things and reveal all the secrets and whatever is essential for my request [state your request] and will not withhold anything from it, because of all the Holy Names that come forth from Psalm 23 and all of the other verses I have recalled and recited before You.

Recite three times:

Amen, Selah.

After completing this prayer, be cautious and refrain from any kind of conversation. Sleep on the left side. Sleep alone in your bed and alone in the house, and be careful to have clean underwear, bed, and sheets. Be careful not to allow your hands to stray below your navel, and do not touch your body. Honor your home by keeping it clean and free from foul odors and anything impure. Above all, one should guard oneself from women and nocturnal pollution.

The customary practice is to compose this request in writing and read from it. After completing everything that has been mentioned, you should then place the request and the prayer under your pillow and concentrate your thoughts upon the request, so that you will fall asleep while contemplating the formulation.

I have developed a variation of the ancient prayer ritual that is more suitable for contemporary men and women. It involves entering a relaxed, meditative state and then presenting one's petition to the Master of Dreams.

Before falling asleep, find a comfortable position in bed and meditate for ten minutes, lying completely still, focusing all of your attention on the relaxed feeling that gradually enters the body as your mind slows down its rapid thinking and a warm, heavy sedation begins to penetrate the entire mind-body. A warm, numb sensation should be gradually experienced as the dominant feeling.

In one form of induced relaxation, which is a variation on the techniques of autogenic training, one begins by reflecting silently and passively with the words "My right arm is heavy" until the sensations are felt. Continue with "My right leg is warm and heavy" . . . "My left leg is warm and heavy" . . . "My left arm is warm and heavy," and so on, ending with "My whole body is warm and heavy." After experiencing the heavy glow of relaxation, say, "My forehead is cool, clear, and relaxed." In this manner, you can mentally observe the flow of relaxation as it circles the body and you fall deeper and deeper into a relaxed state. If you do this exercise every night, a side benefit is that you will learn to enter a relaxed state whenever the need arises during the day as well as at bedtime.

While in this deeply relaxed state, slowly begin addressing the Master of Dreams. Try to remain in the meditative mood while you state your position, and then fall as directly as possible into a restful sleep. If you find that while stating your petition, your adrenaline starts pumping, go back to meditating for a few minutes and then return to stating your petition while remaining in a relaxed state.

The exact form of petitioning the Master of Dreams I leave to the individual. However, the basic mode of the prayer should be a humble petition to some form of the higher self. You may choose to address God, Gabriel, your soul, your spirit guide, or any other inner force, with a clear acceptance and acknowledgment of the limitations of the ego to solve all of one's problems. Feel free to vary your petition as the need arises, but keep the basic form consistent. Developing a proper relationship with your higher self is important if you want to achieve the maximum benefit from your dreams.

One example of addressing the Master of Dreams might be the following:

> Master of Dreams, before I [state your name] enter your world of healing and visions, I place myself at your disposal. I am facing the following concerns and issues that are in need of your guidance. Now I will describe some of my basic concerns for which I need your guidance. . . .

A petition that I have used myself goes something like this:

> Master of Dreams and Psychic Equilibrium, I have been struggling with the following situation and have not been able to

> find the wisdom and insight to assist me in resolving the problem. [State your problem.] I, your humble servant, who feel at the mercy of your greater power and wisdom, place myself in your hands for the night. I beseech you—the fountain of wisdom, insight and healing—to help me find my path. However you appear, whether in the form of an allegory or in any other manner that you want to communicate with me, I will record your communication when I wake, so that it will stay with me and enable me to work at understanding your communication.

In designing your own dream prayer, remember these three key ingredients: One, put yourself in a relaxed state, so that your mind will be more receptive to creative input from your higher self. Two, express, your dependency on the dream for insight. An attitude of humility before the Master of Dreams helps to constellate the inner healer as manifested in the dream. And three, affirm your commitment to remember the dream, record it, and strive for an understanding of its divine message.

Notes

CW in citations refers to C. G. Jung's *Collected Works*, 20 vols. (Princeton, N.J.: Princeton University Press, 1954–1985).

Translations of some of the passages quoted in the text are based on the following English editions, with occasional changes in wording. (In some cases I have translated passages myself.)

Bible: *The Holy Scriptures* (Philadelphia: Jewish Publication Society, 1917).

Talmud: *The Babylonian Talmud*, trans. Maurice Simon, ed. Rabbi Dr. I. Epstein (London: Soncino Press, 1935–1938).

Midrash: *Midrash Rabbah*, trans. Rabbi Dr. H. Freedman, 3rd ed. (London: Soncino Press, 1983).

Zohar: *The Zohar,* trans. Harry Sperling and Maurice Simon, 5 vols. (London: Soncino Press, 1949).

Chapter 1. Dreams in the Jewish Tradition

1. Sigmund Freud, *The Interpretation of Dreams* (New York: Avon Books, 1968), p. 39.

Chapter 3. The Dream as Personal Prophecy

1. *Berakhot* 10b.
2. *Niddah* 30b.
3. Zohar, *Bo.*
4. See Joel Covitz, "A Jewish Myth of A Priori Knowledge," *Spring*, 1971.

5. *Sefer Katnot Or*, quoted in Elijah ben Salomon ha-Kohen, *Midrash Talpiyot* (1698) (Tel Aviv: Leon Offset Press, 1962), p. 139.

6. Talmud, *Sotah* 13b; Midrash, *Exod. Rabbah* 1:24, 26.

7. Talmud, *Pesachim* 118a.

8. See, e.g., Dan. 9:21.

9. Raphael Patai, *Myth and Legend of Ancient Israel*, vol. 3 (New York: Ktav, 1966), p. 184.

10. The visit of the angels is recounted in Gen. 18. The identification of one of the angels as Gabriel is in the Talmud, *Bava Metzia*, 86b.

11. *Exod. Rabbah* 1:26.

12. Joshua Trachtenberg, *Jewish Magic and Superstition* (New York: Atheneum, 1970), p. 234.

13. *Gen. Rabbah* 14:9.

14. Moses Maimonides, *Guide for the Perplexed*, trans. M. Friedlander (New York: Pardes Publishing House, 1946), p. 237.

15. Ibid., p. 243.

16. *Eccles. Rabbah*, 1:2.

17. *Pirke Avot*, 5:25.

18. Heszel Klepfisz, *Culture of Compassion*, trans. Curt Leviant (New York: Ktav, 1983), pp. 105–106.

19. Louis Ginzberg, *The Legends of the Jews*, vol. 1 (Philadelphia: Jewish Publication Society of America, 1909), pp. 275–276.

20. *Pesachim* 64b.

21. *Niddah* 31a.

22. *Berakhot* 55b.

23. *Ta'anit* 21a.

24. *Berakhot* 57b.

25. C. A. Meier, *Ancient Incubation and Modern Psychotherapy* (Evanston, Ill.: Northwestern University Press, 1967), p. 70.

26. *Shabbat* 31b.

27. *CW*8, § 465.

28. See also Joel Covitz, *Emotional Child Abuse* (Boston: Sigo Press, 1986).

29. *Berakhot* 56b.

30. *Yoma* 87b.

31. *Berakhot* 57a.

32. Ibid.

33. *Berakhot* 56b.
34. Freud, *The Interpretation of Dreams*, p. 265.

Chapter 4. The Dream Interpreter

1. *Yoma* 28b.
2. *Berakhot* 55b.
3. Sigmund Freud, *The Interpretation of Dreams* (New York: Avon Books, 1968), p. 130.
4. C. G. Jung, *CW 8, § 539.*
5. Freud, *The Interpretation of Dreams*, p. 388.
6. Robert A. Johnson in C. G. Jung, Emma Jung, and Toni Wolff, *A Collection of Remembrances*, ed. Ferne Jensen (San Francisco: Analytical Psychology Club, 1982), pp. 36–39.
7. *Berakhot* 55b.
8. Milton Erickson, *Advanced Techniques of Hypnosis and Therapy*, Selected Papers of Milton Erickson, ed. Jay Haley (New York: Grune & Stratton, 1967), p. 3.
9. *Bava Batvra 60b; Bava Metzia* 107b.
10. Louis I. Newman, *The Hasidic Anthology* (New York: Bloch Publishing Co., 1944), pp. 83–84.
11. Quoted in Earl A. Grollman, ed., *Rabbinical Counseling* (New York: Block Publishing Co., 1966), p. xvii.
12. Sigmund Freud, *A General Introduction to Psychoanalysis* (New York: Washington Square Press, 1962), p. 241.
13. *The Midrash on Psalms*, trans. William G. Braude (New Haven: Yale University Press, 1959), pp. 429–430.
14. C. G. Jung, *Memories, Dreams, Reflections*, edited and recorded by Aniela Jaffé, trans. Richard and Clara Winston (New York: Vintage Books, 1965), p. 293.
15. Meier, *Ancient Incubation and Modern Psychotherapy*, p. 66.
16. *Berakhot* 56a, b.

Chapter 5. The Art of Positive Dream Interpretation

1. Jung, *CW* 8, § 164.
2. Jung, *CW* 16, § 117–122.
3. Jung, *CW* 18, § 471.

4. Jung, *CW* 17, § 117–122.

5. See also Adolf Guggenbühl-Craig, *Power in the Helping Professions* (Dallas: Spring Publications, 1971).

6. Jung, *Dreams*, vol. 1 (Zurich: The Psychological Club of the C. G. Jung Institute, 1972), p. 65.

7. Quoted in Norman Cousins, *Anatomy of an Illness* (New York: W. W. Norton, 1979), p. 69.

8. Jung, *CW* 17, § 182–183.

9. C. G. Jung, *Modern Man in Search of a Soul* (London: Routledge and Kegan Paul, 1966), p. 223.

10. For more on this subject, see Joel Covitz, "Myth and Money," in Russell A. Lockhart et al., *Soul and Money* (Dallas: Spring Publications, 1982), pp. 63–82.

Chapter 6. Dream Incubation

1. R. J. Zwi Werblowsky, *Joseph Karo: Lawyer and Mystic* (Philadelphia: Jewish Publication Society of America, 1977), pp. 47–48.

2. Joshua Trachtenberg, *Jewish Magic and Superstition* (New York: Atheneum, 1970), pp. 242–243.

Glossary of Jewish Terms

Adonai. One of the names of God. In Hebrew it literally means "my Lord." The name is considered holy by religious Jews, who pronounce it only during prayer or when reading the Bible.

Ark of the Covenant. The original wooden chest containing the sacred tablets inscribed with the Ten Commandments, once housed in the Holy Temple in Jerusalem.

Chasidic. Referring to the Chasidim (literally, "pious ones"), members of a mystical religious movement that began among eastern European Jews in the eighteenth century.

Diaspora. The countries outside of Israel where Jews reside since their exile from the Holy Land.

El. One of the names of God.

Elohim. One of the names of God. In some passages the word can refer not to the Deity but to angels, gods, rulers, or judges, i.e., any superior power or powers.

Holy Temple. The Temple in Jerusalem where the Jews worshiped in ancient times. The First Temple, built by Solomon, was destroyed by Nebuchadnezzar in 586 B.C.E. The Second Temple was destroyed by the Romans in 70 C.E.

Kabbalist. A proponent of Kabbalah, the Jewish mystical tradition, which flourished in the fifteenth and sixteenth centuries.

Midrash. Generic term for collected commentaries on the Bible. The *midrashim* (plural of *midrash*) are nonlegalistic teachings relating to legends, sayings, and moralisms.

Pirke Avot. ("Sayings of the Fathers") A collection of moral teachings from the Mishnah.

Prophets. The second section of three in the Hebrew Bible, including such books as Isaiah, Jeremiah, and Ezekiel. The other two sections are the Torah and the Writings.

rebbe. A Chasidic master.

Sefer Chasidim ("Book of the Pious"). A book of folklore, anecdotes, and legends written by Rabbi Yehudah ha-Chasid in the thirteenth century.

sefirah. One of the ten "emanations" or aspects of God's Being, according to the Kabbalists.

Shaddai. One of the names of God.

Shekhinah. The Divine Presence, a feminine aspect of God.

Shema. The prayer expressing Judaism's belief in the unity of God, recited twice a day, morning and evening. It is customary to say the Shema at bedtime.

Talmud. A huge compendium of commentaries on the Torah by rabbinical scholars. The term generally refers to the Babylonian Talmud, which was recorded between the third and fifth centuries C.E.

Torah. The Five Books of Moses (Genesis, Exodus, Leviticus, Numbers, and Deuteronomy). More broadly, all of Jewish Law.

tzaddikim (singular, *tzaddik*). Literally, "righteous ones"; saints or holy men of Judaism.

Urim and Tumim. An oracle in the days of the Holy Temple, worn on the high priest's breastplate, which conveyed God's will to the people of Israel.

Writings. The section of the Hebrew Bible including Psalms, Proverbs, Song of Songs, Ruth, Esther, etc.

Yahweh. A rendering of the sacred name of God consisting of four Hebrew letters. This name is never pronounced as spelled by religious Jews; the name Adonai is substituted for it in prayer.

Zohar. The *Sefer ha-Zohar* ("Book of Splendor"), the most important kabbalistic text, attributed to the second-century rabbi Simeon bar Yohai but probably written in the thirteenth century by the Spanish rabbi Moses de Leon.